T0162334

ERRANÇITIES

Errançities

POEMS

Quincy Troupe

COFFEE HOUSE PRESS
MINNEAPOLIS
2012

Coffee House Press books are available to the trade through our primary distributor, Consortium Book Sales & Distribution, www.cbsd.com or (800) 283-3572. For personal orders, catalogs, or other information, write to: info@coffeehousepress.org.

Coffee House Press is a nonprofit literary publishing house. Support from private foundations, corporate giving programs, government programs, and generous individuals helps make the publication of our books possible. We gratefully acknowledge their support in detail in the back of this book. To you and our many readers around the world, we send our thanks for your continuing support.

Good books are brewing at www.coffeehousepress.org

LIBRARY OF CONGRESS CATALOGING-IN-PUBLICATION DATA
Troupe, Quincy.
Errançities : new poems 2006 to 2010 / by Quincy Troupe.
p. cm.
ISBN 978-1-56689-283-4 (alk. paper) cloth
ISBN 978-1-56689-276-6 (pbk : alk. paper) paperback
I. Title.
PS3570.R63E77 2012
811'.54—dc23
2011031384

Printed in Canada
1 3 5 7 9 8 6 4 2
FIRST EDITION | FIRST PRINTING

ACKNOWLEDGMENTS
Some of these poems first appeared in the following anthologies, journals, and magazines: *Asheville Poetry Review, Coon Bidness – SO 4sulfate, Drumvoices Revue, Legardo: Fliporto 2008, Let Loose on the World: Celebrating Amiri Baraka at 75, Mission at Tenth, NeoHoodoo: Art for a Forgotten Faith, phati'tude, Platte River Review,* and *The Spoken Word Workbook.*

For my wife, Margaret Porter Troupe,
and my mother, Dorothy Smith Marshall,
as always in gratitude.

For Hamiet Bluiett, Kelvyn Bell, Allison Hedge Coke,
Victor Hernández Cruz, Janet Gaertner, K. Curtis Lyle, Walter and Teresa
Sanchez Gordon, Mildred Howard,
Oliver Jackson, Eugene B. Redmond, Ishmael Reed,
Peter N. G. Schwartz, Donald Suggs, Donald Troupe, and
John Edgar Wideman for their friendship
and support over all these long years.

For my agent Jennifer Gates,
and my publisher and editor, Allan Kornblum.

And to the memory of Alexander Skunder Boghossian,
Aimé Césaire,. Lucille Clifton, Miles Davis, Edouard Glissant,
Al Loving, and Sekou Sundiata: may their creative contributions always be
remembered and their souls rest in peace.

1

2

3

4

5

6

7

Note Regarding the Title

Errance is a French word that means "to wander," or "a roving, wandering life" It can also mean "a risky, edgy, wandering life." I first discovered the word while reading the poems of Edouard Glissant, the late distinguished poet, philosopher, novelist, and critical thinker from Martinique. I fell in love with the word and its meaning, and it seemed to apply to my life and the poems I was writing at the time, many of which have found their way into this new volume. But, although I love the word *errance* and what it meant, I felt it wasn't exactly what I needed. So, I coined the neologism *errançities,* an expression I felt more at home with, especially in the way the new word sounded, rolled off my tongue. The rhythm of *errançities* was closer to another neologism of mine, *Trancircularities,* which was the title of my seventh book of poems, published by Coffee House in 2002. Also, in my mind, *errançities* means plural wanderings of many lives, rather than one life. Thus, *Errançities* is the title of this new book of poems. I hope you enjoy some of them.

—QUINCY TROUPE, FEBRUARY 2011

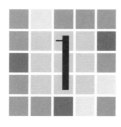

An Art of Lost Faith

for Robert Farris Thompson, Maya Deren & Ishmael Reed

I. BEGINNINGS: A PLACE OF SILENCE
in a place beyond our knowing, silence reigns, darkness
perhaps, some light, echoes, in this vast space,
perhaps it is a netherworld, an etherworld of maybe,
if spirits amongst us know what *It* is, they have never spoken,
perhaps shadows have, over/underground in some invisible space,
surrounded by air, water, where spirits of creation exist,
swimming or zooming outside our comprehension,
a place where only imagination through prayer can take us,
to a road, perhaps, a passageway stretching long & far,
deep into the past, perhaps, a doorway leading to nowhere,
nobody knows, only silence knows the language echoes speak
in this vast place beyond knowing, are bones, teeth, hair,
ribcages, skulls, toes, fingers here, are maggots here, too,
do they speak some kind of music in this beyond world,
do they understand silence, the twilight world of myth, memory
of water, earth, sky, wind, the memory of fire, earthquakes, thunder,
the memory of storms, lightning, ice, the memory of creation,
birth, death, the memory of everything here & gone, everywhere
a mystery, is what we know is certain, an idea of something
without shape or form, pulsating with what we know is power,
It is a metaphysical presence, a blessing with what we know
is the ability to heal & destroy this space we live in
only by *Its* invitation, sanction, only by *Its* blessing,
this place we've been born into with so much amnesia

2. LOOKING THROUGH MIST TOWARD AFRICA

in the beginning was a sound, a crack of light, fissure in the dark
dome of the sky, earth, from which a resonance of air echoed,
perhaps something like a note, a sudden sound,
or wind moving toward expression, a beginning, a seed of language,
perhaps, a hum, a grunt moving toward something clearer, perhaps
a voice, which became visible, later, as a stroke of whatever was needed
at the time, some kind of music, beating like a heart
in time with a first act of gesture, imitating a shaking
in the ground, something close to a rhythm,
a grain of language, something like a word, perhaps a growl, something
the ears of earth, air & sky might hear & know what was coming was
a kind of improvisation, a phenomenal act of creation,
perhaps shadows in a garden, under what we know now are iroko trees,
moving the way humans would, fusing memories, music
in a beautiful rhythm, undulating, coming together,
moving apart, in an act of expression we know as joy,
perhaps, love, a feeling of ecstasy, an act of vital conception,
invention, making, in fact, an act of copulation,
in the holy Yoruba city of Ile-Ife, where Olorun, god of all things Yoruba,
(*the* vital force, neither male or female, the ultimate embodiment of *ashé,*
spiritual command, the power to make-things-happen)
slithered down from the sky in the form of a royal python snake,
bringing with *It, Eshu, Ogun, Yemoja, Oshun, Oshoosi,*
Obaluaiye, Shango, Obatala, Oko, Egungun, bringing
the power to give life, take life away, *ashé, ashé, ashé*
as an earthworm, white snail, woodpecker, gaboon viper,
ashé represented by iron staffs, long-beaked birds, iron sculptures
of serpents in the form of kings, chiefs, wise old women
coming in the form of birds, sacred beads on the crowns of kings
hanging from their masks, covering their faces during moments of prophecy,

ritualized during times of possession, *ashé*
in these forces watching us through spiritual eyes,
with the power to give life, take life away, *ashé*
on an old ceramic bowl, *It* is the thunder of Shango,
a meandering pattern of pythons, gaboon vipers twisting through sand,
lightning zigzagging through space, unzipping the black bowl of the sky
above an iroko tree, its trunk tied with white cloth as an offering,
semen at its base, drops of blood sprinkled around it too,
is a gift to the gods, as a person dressed in red is *ashé*

then everything was lost in sandstorms of confusion, tribal rivalries,
blood spilling reduced to ashes civilizations of prophecy,
divinations began to lose images of faith after Europeans arrived
with greed in their eyes, storming off ships guns spitting fire,
carried away priests, their faith, across middle passage to the New World,
though these chained holy men still whispered under their breath the holy word
ashé, ashé, ashé, the rhythms of talking drums held tight in memory,
on wide seas, in the sky lightning flashed, kaboom, gunfire, *ashé,*
then silence

3. THE NEW WORLD

many priests died during the middle passage, shot, whipped dead,
their bodies thrown to sharks in the roiling salt water,
when survivors arrived in the New World *ashé* was a memory
under their breath, the tempo of talking drums transformed to something new
though it kept old roots beating close to the rhythm of hearts. Gods changed, too,
transformed through language, African prayer fused with Native American Indian,
French & Spanish ones, too, *ashé* grew new animating forces,
loas, houngans—priests—stirred the pot, rediscovered powers over the soul,
spirit, self, bloomed as new voodoo avatars anchored in old ways though

transformed here into new ways of bringing spirits down,
in this new world all manner of tribes, races, metamorphosed into creole
cultures—languages, faiths, music—old drum rhythms innovated new accents,
added them to ancient measures, fused into newfangled tempos,
married fresh New World time signatures—Congo rhythms birthed Petro beats,
music/dance of Rara, compass, Rada songs from Dahomey—
visual arts expressed through shimmering voodoo flags holding mirrors
reflecting souls in lakes of glass—whispering poetic rituals of *ashé*
married Catholic, indigenous Native American Indian religious mantras,
the dead began serving the living, ritual became reclamation of the soul,
everything was transformed as night sounds cooed, undulating
sweetness found in mangoes, papayas, red flesh of watermelons
unlocked primal mysteries as hurricanes howled & swirled,
Veves invoked *loas,* retainers of the vital force, miracle fireflies
of spiritual command, the power-to-make-things-happen,
bestow life & take life away through possession,
black seeds of language loomed in the fresh silence

4. SOLO
I have come to this text to sing the gospel of Neo-Hoodoo,
the rediscovery of self in this new, cruel whirl
of dilettantes seeking greed through senseless wars, who machine
gun down any spirit who can dance words across empty white pages,
who refuse to recognize any culture save their own as a vital force
in the world, who speak with forked tongues,
who think they know everything when their history is so short
& bloody, charlatans who raze the world with bombs, spitting bullets,
whose religion is greed, who cannot hear wisdom or music,
whose time is finally short, whose storehouse of stolen ideas is empty,
whose ragtag culture of hobos went up in flames like so much in the West,

many of us are here now, have been transformed through memory of *ashe,*
its drum rhythms synonymous with our own beating hearts,
we know the lost faith—now recovered—as our own vital force, its syncopations
reborn in Voodoo/Santeria/Candomble/Neo-Hoodoo in the New World,
we got High John the Conqueror in lines of our poetry, got mojo hands
guiding brushstrokes of our paintings, Papa Ogun in our sculpture,
Yoruba/Petro rhythms infusing blues, spirituals, ragtime, gospel, jazz,
merengue, salsa, rhythm 'n' blues, rhumba, tango, zouk,
soul, rock 'n' roll & rap, we move our feet & bodies to dance
entranced with recovered rhythms of a lost faith, infused here
in art of a New World expression probing deep,
it connects us to an ancestral faith we embrace here as our own
magic, mystery, power, grace, expressed through our hearts
as an ever-evolving, powerful, Neo-Hoodoo expression, voiced through priests
like james brown, sly stone, miles davis, jimi hendrix, charlie parker,
thelonious monk & marie laveau, voiced through every man, woman
viewing themselves as sacred innovators, improvisers of the spiritual body dance,
the art of a lost faith is not lost when reinterpreted, is everything
griots & shamans know to be real on earth, surrounded by air,
phenomenological, Voodoo transformed to Neo-Hoodoo here,
transplanted in the New World space with magic, faith of the Old World,
American fusion is iconography rooted in the new/old transmogrification,
a logo for America, perhaps, a pathway to a future of the new, Neo-
Hoodoo, perhaps found through the words, *ashé, ashé, ashé,*
is perhaps a fresh, innovative life-force gathering in the air

When Time Was Young

in the beginning no one knew what the beginning was
what force act what mad genius pulled the trigger
shooting time into space was a commencement an inauguration
all of this was in fact true was an installation a swearing-in drama
& time in the opening act was perhaps dressed up as a bird
was all in feathers & flew where nobody had a clue
though all unheard voices from then say it became
a silent language when anything open tried to breathe
attempting to speak a blue cloud whispered a pulse of hushed
utterance slipped out became a newfangled mode of communication
only circling hawks understood the frequency of before time did
a boogie-woogie shuffled folded its wings dove back down
into the dazzling hole it flew out of in the first place as a breeze-
licked petal trembled as though it was an unmanned boat
floating on still waters of a lake somewhere under the sun

& it was bright before anyone knew the beginning of sound
was time light a short period measured by intervals
a second a slice a beat in the duration of speed & space
though some segments had no sense of rhythm were caught up in blind
spots gaps in the yah-de-yah-da power of crows who were colophons
fixed somewhere in memory perched high up in cerulean air
where some were seen blowing smoke signals through large beaks
like etchings of black men wearing headdresses of indian feathers
when this poem flashed forward to see
mardi gras flowing magical scenes through old new orleans streets

before katrina came sweeping everything away in loop de loops
of wind rain violent swirling water the stupidity of avaricious men
silencing for a while all that wondrous music african-indian tribes created
dancing strutting up a storm through neo-hoodoo beats of new orleans

then the storms of amnesia tore up the original roadmap
& we found ourselves navigating inside our own frazzled brains
now some of us find our spirits wandering around tasting cobalt
chemicals on our tongues sluicing through our minds
as time pulsed beats between two sapphire stones
at opposite ends of the world we bore witness before a black
swirling cloud dropped down howling from the yellow sky

it was the moment some of us finally knew the beginning of time
was the vanishing of light fleeing gloom of those days without heartbeats

& we never understood why we never heard the trembling whisper before
the howling raised at that precise moment of our terror why no one knew
the truth of light leaving was in fact the beginning of all
the silence of all the dark days that were poised to come

Las Cruces, New Mexico Revisited

for Keith Wilson, Donna Epps Ramsey, Andrew Wall, Charles Thomas
& Thomas Hocksema

I.

you have come to this space of light & pure beauty
from the love-song tongues of ancestors ringing
you have risen from an earth soaked in human blood
animal blood bird blood fish blood slicking polluted water
singing the gospel you have bloomed like a desert flower
under the cross of crucifixion your pain deep as poetry
river deep pure as love flowing back to jordan
blood-holy from africa you have come reborn to us
with the spirit of healing you cleanse us now
baptize us in clear water of your sun-warm words
& you have carried the holy flame of god through stone rain
kept it burning like a candle in the church of your heart
& you have kept the faith with your holy gods with jesus
with malcolm with martin luther king in everyman
& you have come wearing the mantle of adam
your own sermon on the mount in your own throat
O gentle native man luminous with tenderness
your commitment your faith in love is so very holy beautiful
as the spirit of ancestors tonguing through your blood
their pain veining river-deep through your gospel of holy feathers
your sacred text of healing deep singing in your sacred mountains
your sermons bringing us here to this clear sweetness of place
to this space this moment where you are light & beauty
your words drum-scripts we hear see in your dance steps
carried in hearts throughout the world where you live

2.

eye have come here to these sacred great mesas high up above
las cruces to sit meditate on this land flat as vegas gambling tables
rock-hard as red dust swirls into miniature tornados
dancing down roads red with silence silent as the faces of solitary
indians here where white men quick-tricked
their way to power with hidden agendas
of bullets & schemes of false treaties
& black men alone here in this stark high place of mesquite
bushes white sand mountains colors snapped in incredible
beauty eyes walking down vivid sunsets livid purple scars slashing
volcanic rock tomahawking language scalping this ruptured space
of forgotten teepees so eye listen to a coyote wind
howling & yapping across the cactused dry high vistas
kicking up skirts of red dirt at the rear end of quiet houses
squatting like dark frogs & crows etched silhouettes high on live
wires popping speech caw-cawing in the sandblasted wind
stroked trees caw-cawing all over the mesilla valley

& here along the rio grande river dry, parched tongue bed snaking
mud cracked & dammed north in the throat of albuquerque
mescalara zuni apache & navaho live here
scratch out their firewater breath peyote
secret eyes roaming up & down these gaming-table mesas
their memories dragging chains through these red breathing streets
while geronimo's raging ghost haunts their lives with what
they did not do stretching this death-strewn history back
to promises & hope a hole in the sky a red omen moon
where death ran through like water whirlpooling down a sink

& this shaman moon a red target of light at the end
of a tunnel of blackness where a train speeds through now
towing breakneck flights of light where daybreak sits wrapped
like a blanket around a quiet ancient navaho wrapped in american colors
who sits meditating these scorched white sands flat distant high mesas
shaped like royal "basotho hats" chili peppers churls
pecan groves roadrunners chaparral birds salt cedars sprouting
parasitic along bone-white ditches bordering riverbeds thirsting for water
meditates these wide flat black lava rocks holding strange imprints
of fossilized speech that died before it knew what hit it
as did those silent clay-faced ancestors of this solitary navaho sitting here
wrapped in breaking colors bursting sunlight meditating the lay
of this enchanting blues land changing its face every mile or so

& in their faces indians carry the sadness of ancestors
who wished they had listened to those long gone
flaming words—battlecries!—of geronimo, whose screaming ghost
prowls these bloody muddy streets baked dry now by the flaming eye
torching the sky wished they had listened instead of chaining
his message in these coyote howling winds kicking up skirts of dirt
whose language yaps like toothless old men & women
squatting at the rear end of quiet houses whose lights dance slack
at midnight grow black & silent as death's worn-out breath
beneath these pipe-organ mountains bishop's peaked caps
holding incredible silence here in the mesilla valley
where the rio grande river runs dry
its thirsty spirit dammed north in the throat of albuquerque
at the crossroads of fusion & silence in the red gush swirls—

whispering litanies sawblading through ribcages dust memories—
snaking winds tonguing over the mesilla valley brings back
long-gone words of geronimo haunting las cruces new mexico
long-gone wind whispering geronimo geronimo geronimo

NOTE: When I was putting together my work for *Skulls Along the River* (I Reed Books, 1984), I discovered that I had lost the first part of this poem. But I liked what I had at the time, and decided to include it in the book. When Coffee House Press published *Transcircularities: New and Selected Poems* in 2002, I did a little rewriting, and included the revised version. Finally, on September 21, 2009, I found the original text of *Las Cruces, New Mexico* with the original "part one," added it to the rest of the text, and then revisited and revised the entire poem to make it into a single, new piece, published here at last.

Going Back to Voices Lost in the Past

when eye go back to visit "sad louis," dumped on the mississippi river
eye encounter ghost faces haunting my childhood memories there
as if they were forgotten gloomy buildings barely standing,
most things seemed so much happier back then—
fifty years ago—than they do now, when all of us seemed blessed
with young bright faces, sleek strong bodies, all our lives up ahead of us
seemed so filled with unlimited promise then, now, today
when eye walk into a rundown juke joint in the old neighborhood,
hear strains of chuck berry, albert king thumping out rhythms & lyrics—
still good enough for my ears—from an old jukebox time forgot,

eye see shadows of people leaning into their sorrows
perched like broken-wing birds on rickety stools—substituting for branches—
heads hung over an ancient wooden bar, razor-sharp splinters pricking
their fingers, drawing drops of blood,
they look so hamscammy now, their faces sagging—like mine—
look like ruined buildings waiting for the wrecking ball,

but eye have come back here to see them, catch up on their lives,
their bodies—like mine, too—mirror heartbreaking ruin,

eye see the bartender's sunken wizened face—because of shrunken gums,
lost teeth—grin at me, hinting recognition, perhaps dredging up my face
from some place buried deep in his cobwebbed memory—
perhaps it is some semblance of it, a vague outline suddenly jumping out at him
in a flash from some hidden crevice he has excavated—maybe he recalls

a recent photo fading in a newspaper advertising me coming back to town
to read poetry, or do something else people like me do to make do,
perhaps he only thinks he knows me—though
eye can't remember his name at all but acknowledge his face nodding my head
back at him like eye was taught to do growing up, in recognition of him
maybe recognizing me—eye don't know what else to do, what

can eye say—it's getting dicey these days in situations like this,
because people might think you dissing them when you don't acknowledge
who they are (never mind people most likely look like somebody else
you thought you knew from some other place, in some other time), after all
few of us still look like we used to—we're either bigger than a house
or shrunken like we been stricken with cancer—
given the fact it's been so long since we laid eyes on each other,
plus our memory done slipped more than a notch—being nowhere near
what it used to be—so why do people get pissed off,
get their asses up on their shoulders when someone doesn't recognize them
despite all this blooming fog years done brought between us now,
clouding up all our memories, still it ain't no telling how
people might react during bad times like these, with all these lethal
weapons spread around, going *pop pop pop* everywhere
you turn—nobody's life worth a plugged wooden nickel these days,

so eye give the bartender some props when eye nod at him,
he nods back at me, too, perhaps recognizing we both living inside
our own slippery, fading, in & out moments of memory,

so why not just have a drink, share in the miracle we are still here, now,
can celebrate during these few moments we have left with each other,
enjoy the memories, the fellowship of times long gone,
never to be repeated, revel in even the lies we will tell each other—

they are precious—spend them like good money with each other,
for the good times we had together, when our bodies were young,
sleek, strong, our faces so bright with promise,

eye *should* be here with them for these moments,
perhaps for the very last time before we all become ghosts,
in time reduced to fragments of speech, our spirits left behind
perhaps in memories of others—if at all—
perhaps to haunt this poem, if & when someone reads it, or hears
the words of our lives slipped off someone's tongue floating orally

in the polluted air, before wasting away like falling ashes

Historic Attitudes in Birds (& Humans)

we left a plate of brown sugar on our table
at beausejour restaurant, high in the mountains
above pointe-noire, guadeloupe, the caribbean sea
fronting us to the west, an hour before sunset,

soon a flock of yellow-breasted sucrier birds
flew down, began eating sugar until they were full,
looking out for the jet-black hunter cat
skulking around tables, looking for food,

shortly a black sucrier tried joining the ones
with yellow breasts feasting on sugar, but it was chased,
perhaps because of its color, who knows what

weird things go on inside heads of birds & people,
certainly not me, eye have to deal with my own vexing
problems, way too many to write about here

Where Have They All Gone

for Ojenke, Eric Priestley & K. Curtis Lyle

where have they all gone to, those exuberant edgy misfits,
those glorious madcap poets of precise inexactitude,
those lunatic purveyors of transcendental flights through space,
verbal high jinks sky walkers of jazzified hyperbolic scatology,
rhapsodic sleepwalkers selling screaming jay hawkins wolf tickets,
echoing skull & bone dances of dahomey voodoo smack downs,
emanating from beyond watery graves of middle passage,
from the genocide of millions

all the spiritual six-fingered witch doctors brewing up revenge
secreted deep in hidden holes of linguistic thoroughfares,
those sacred red-robed wilt chamberlain maasai spiritual hunters,
who chase hunters of lions running free around ngorongoro, tanzania,

eye say, where have all the stork-legged soothsayer space cadets
traveled to, disciples of sun ra's bamboozling cloudbursts of words,
those smoke signal purveyors of mojo language hypnotized
through music,

those schizophrenic soothsayers practicing loop-de-loop tom-toms,
rhythmic scavengers of esoteric metaphors stitched throughout
knuckleheaded sentences, illuminated by yardbird parker
excursions through solos exploring outer limits of scatological space,
thelonious monk comping along as acoustical solar sidekick,
riffin' off only he knows what "mysterioso" piano licks,

where have they all gone to, those insane rollerblade skaters
decked out in silver asbestos suits & caps, wraparound shades,
zooming, weaving through manhattan traffic like lone ranger silver
bullets, those slingshot word magicians, loup-garou wordsmiths
shooting out rhythms hidden deep in thickets of reared-back cobra
tongues, who flick out hypnotic spells, undulating spellbinding
tempos at seductive dances, where beautiful full breasts
bob up & down like ripe melons, seducing like honey,
lips dripping with sweet lusting desire, licking, sucking kisses,
tongues probing mouths when passion sweeps down overwhelming
the senses, as when in cunnilingus her body trembles, explodes,

where has pamela donegan gone to with her deep-loving-holy-
gripping-sweet-seductive-suction-cup that caused men to howl
anytime they came with her, like mad wolves celebrating the moon,
where has leumas sirrah (samuel harris spelled backwards)
disappeared to, who sat upon rooftops all over watts sniffing glue,
talking shit to the sun & writing incomprehensible beautiful poetry,
what about stilt-legged, tall & skinny, midnight-blue emory evans,
from north carolina, who walked around watts wearing a long,
navy-blue wool overcoat in 95 degree weather,
wore high-top, black tennis shoes & wrote love poems to ants
& broken-winged birds & everything that moved or didn't move,
where have clyde mays & cleveland sims gone to
with their criminal schemes & quixotic over-the-top poems,

as our lives unfold, switch, turn with cycles of sun & moon,
seconds turn into minutes into hours into days into years,
people, scenes, events, time becomes history erased from memory
if not recorded, written down (even then some fall through

cracks or holes in narratives, fall victim to amnesia, or even worse—
alzheimer's, where memory falls down into a black hole, is erased—

so where have all those exuberant, edgy misfits gone,
those glorious madcap poets of precise inexactitude, lunatic
purveyors of transcendental flights through space, verbal high jinks
sky walkers of jazzified hyperbolic scatology, grace,
rhapsodic sleepwalkers selling screaming jay hawkins wolf tickets,
echoing skull & bone dances of dahomey voodoo smack downs,
emanating from beyond watery graves of middle passage, space,

where have all the spiritual six-fingered witch doctors gone
whose spirits could not be locked up in a jar, or even poetry,
have they all gone to chasing erranceties, errançities,
the sun, moon & stars inside their heads even underground?

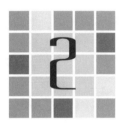

Harlem: Circa 1983—1984

I.

there were hooded black specters everywhere eye looked,
imagine visiting the greek mythic underworld of hades,
a space for the living dead, it was here back then, all over harlem,
hooded black men drooping to their knees like limp stems of flowers
huddled around oil drums rusted brown as their pallid skin,
warming their hands over bouquets of flames shooting up from those oil drums
any season—winter, spring, summer, autumn—during those wicked years—
though my memories of these terrible scenes seem mostly in frigid winter—
it was hell to pay walking these streets back then
amongst those hooded specters sagging into death dances
everywhere they stood from constantly shooting heroin—white death—
into their bloated popeye arms hands feet & legs scarred by needle tracks, pus-
        holes, blooming aids, then there were these other new specters scurrying
        around like roaches
in filthy dark crack dens when lights came on, eyes feverish
as rabid dogs ignited to move after sucking on crack pipes—also white death—
scenes right out of a mad max movie—every day eye saw bonfires in dewy square—
renamed A. Phillip Randolph Square today—from my seventh-floor window,
blooming in central harlem, like large, tropical, orange flowers

2.

back in the day, 1945, bird used to come to get high in dewy square
on a break from playing minton's, the great jazz club right around the corner,
where monk used to tickle ivory keys into a new language, while dizzy shot
incredible trumpet flights on his bent golden horn into space,

35

while a young miles davis watched, shaking his head absorbing everything,
awed by all the genius music played in this temple of sound, baby
lawrence tap dancing out on the sidewalk in front of the club for free—

that was then—this is now, circa 1983, '84, the whole block of 116th street,
between Seventh & Eighth Avenues, lined with blazing rusted oil drums
every night, hooded black specters hovering feverishly, scanning the scene,
darting bullet eyes looking for victims when they need a fix,
always, every day, until they come to their senses, kick the habit,
or melt away like snow in springtime when the sun comes up

Amnesia #1

everywhere many people seem to have forgotten everything,
they walk amongst wavering shadows of themselves,
snaking across landscapes, do they remember anything
they lived through but believe only what's up on hollywood/tv
screens, do they really have even a clue what history can teach them
about senseless endless wars leaving real bodies bloody & dead
on destroyed city streets as rerun souvenirs from propaganda,
fake movies sluicing through their out-of-touch brains
while many real war veterans wake up—many homeless—
screaming in the suffocating nights, terrified at the carnage
their dittoing ignorance & zealotry created, left behind,
in countless places ruined across a devastated planet

Amnesia #2: Three White Men Sit in a Row on a Subway Train

three white men sit in a row across from me riding
the uptown number 3 train in new york city,
they are wearing expensive suits, white shirts & ties,
rolex watches, beautiful, to-die-for italian shoes,
they carry soft leather attaché cases
stuffed with god-only-knows what kind of paper information,
perhaps controlling the lives of countless

people, whose rate of heartbeats, anxiety these men might have
jerked now & again, according to *their* needs, *their* whims,
their fluctuating appetites of greed, *their* florescent egos,
what they wanted at any given moment was once *theirs*
simply because in *their* minds it was *their* privilege to have
because of skin color, the texture of their hair,
the tint of arrogance in their eyes that comes
with their genealogy, their breeding,
all stamped into their passport of dispensation,

today though their eyes look down at the train floor flummoxed,
they are surrounded by people they have never known, never had to know,
today these men across from me seem to be asking themselves "why
are we here instead of riding like the kings we are in the sleek
limousines we have always ridden in since we can remember"

in the past their actions were like unmanned fire hoses
spraying water into the air, out of control, using other people's money

down on wall street, all their financial whims seemed like sure bets
that would keep the greenbacks gushing
like black gold, pouring into *their* bank accounts—they thought,
all *their* wildest dreams would *never* end

but here they are, looking like war-torn refugees
who barely escaped with the clothes on their back
from the disaster of wall street after the flaming point drop—
a 777-point plunge—of stocks crashed & burned,
zapped peoples' brains to goo after that monday full of tears—
september 29, 2008—when many dreams went up in flames—
did these three men across from me forget what goes up
must come down & everyone here on earth is human?

look at them slumped across from me,
former masters of the universe, mammon worshipers,
beelzebufos, gamblers—they look as if they've lost everything—
perhaps they have—shock written all over their body language,
shock registered everywhere in their drawn faces
drained of all arrogance, their certainty suddenly broken
like crystal goblets shattering to smithereens
when dropped on a black marble floor

Amnesia #3: Photographs & Videos

looking at snapshots in a photo book eye remember seeing people
like these before, their ordinary, plain blank faces,
flat in black & white photographs, gazing out vacantly
through blue eyes, or gray, or black as small bores, or pebbles,
dumb as local stones found littering the ground where they stand now
underneath these trees, where they are gathered
as if for a picnic in these fading photographs
in this book, or others like this one, stored away in vaults,
in yellowing pages of tattered old newspapers
& in the pictures the people don't seem to notice the body—though
some seem to have a hint or flicker of a smile playing
around the corners of their lips thin as wires, while others point
their fingers absentmindedly upward toward the "strange fruit" hanging
grotesquely above their heads from a tree branch, or the carcass,
charred beyond recognition of anything human,
resting on smoking embers on the scorched bier in front of them—
but how could they not notice the acrid smell
of burnt flesh, the screaming, toxic stench, the excrement released
at the moment when the rope snapped the neck at the spinal cord
& death kicked in, in a spasm of twitching,
herky-jerky trembling of the body, the eyes popping out,
the tongue protruding, lolling from the now slack mouth—
didn't this now passive crowd—they were raucous before
the shadow-catcher's shutter caught them
demurely posing—smell this awful stench of death?

that was then, this is now & we see these look-alike faces once again,
in october 2008, though rage has replaced the stillness in those
aged daguerreotypes, perhaps we are looking at descendents of people
snapped in those old photographs—so silent then when caught
on camera—screaming bloody murder now
at republican presidential rallies for john mccain & sarah palin,
during boiling tea party rallies in august 2009, who *all* hate another black man,
this time the forty-fourth president of these yet to be united states,
this time modern videos & microphones caught their remarkable rage,
their fist-thrusting, hate-filled images & voices for history,
which informs us, lets us know very little has changed

After Seeing an Image in Ashland, Oregon

a full moon stares like a one-eyed panther's surprised
good eye, bright over ashland, oregon,
$\qquad\qquad\qquad\qquad$ hangs in space
a gleaming silver dollar
$\qquad\qquad\qquad$ stamped into the skin of midnight
$\qquad\qquad\qquad\qquad\qquad\qquad$ & is a hole
punched clear through to the other side of dreaming,
where light is pulsating energy,
wide open as surprise, a flashlight beaming
one ray brighter than faith, is a reflection of what
we see hanging there,
$\qquad\qquad$ complete in this moment,

$\qquad\qquad\qquad\qquad$ the twin good eye opposite a blind one,

veiled in darkness black as othello's human though
demon dream, struggling to cut loose all that anchoring baggage
connected to skin tone, all these weighted syllables

words serve as glue to bond narratives
stitched with flawed images, metaphors filling history,
as its narrative stumbles forward stereo loud
as those false coon-shows typically slurping,
devouring good-old sweet watermelons, red-lipped

& scratching on green manicured, white suburban lawns

On a Sunday

for Amiri Baraka

eye remember seeing the oblong fruit—mango,
papaya—in a photo of a lynched black man's

head fixed above the exclamation point of his tad-
pole body, swaying easy in a tree in a gentle

breeze, it is summer in my memory, warm,
not yet swelteringly hot in southern steel country

alabama, outside birmingham, where
john coltrane blew hauntingly of four little black girls

blown to smithereens on a sunday, in church,
eye also remember hearing chuck berry playing guitar

on a sunday, in the back seat of his white cadillac car,
driven by his red-haired black wife, cruising st. louis

blues streets, singing, "roll over beethoven,
tell tchaikovsky the news, there's a new kind

of music called rhythm 'n' blues," on that sunday
the sky was blue as it was in my memory—

where all things are elusively fixed,
because nothing is ever permanent save change—

cobalt blue, sapphire blue, cerulean blue
when eye saw the lynched man's head in the photograph

oblique above the exclamation point of his tadpole body,
it was a sapphire-blue sunday in the deep freeze

of january, when barack obama
took the oath of office, became the forty-fourth

president of this divided nation in crisis,
the voices of reason were thrown out the window

like bathwater, soap, an infant in a small plastic tub,
a bawling baby hitting the ground, breath atomized

as vaporizing matter, misted into the air in a fog
like an elegy, a sunday listening to punditry talking—

points hitting the fan on TV screens, their elegies
leering all over the planet, richly paid for drivel,

their infested dialogue, their blather like plagues,
prattling disinformation, sluiced through airwaves,

zapping clueless people inside their atomized brains,
glued, as they are, to these talking heads flashing

expensive dental-wear as they natter their shopworn
rhetoric into cameras, connecting us to them

through plasma TV screens, on glory bird sundays
& the blues as a way of life everywhere, even on sundays

when all things are elusively fixed, even words of sermons,
because nothing is ever permanent save change,

the sky sometimes blue as a sapphire woman
wearing red, her hips moving from side to side, beckoning

with her sensuous, sashaying hips, come-to-me-poppa strut,
seducing where the gospel of sweetness is elusively fixed

inside a church, a juke joint, the music hot as her allure,
hittin' it, layin' the mojo down, conjurin' up wicked

spirits, as poets raising the roof from its foundation up
into cerulean-blue, sapphire-blue, cobalt-blue air,

preachers running the gospel down on sundays with their
sermons everywhere, people living inside their memories,

where all things are elusively fixed, but here
nothing is ever permanent save change after change

nothing is ever permanent save change

Mix-y-uppy Memory

eye got on the uptown c train traveling north to harlem,
the day was beautiful up-top over ground, down here
on the subway eye pass a funky black man swaddled in rags
sitting in the car where eye choose to rest my tropical spirit
filled with dreams of mangoes, papayas, the sweet space
my wife's delectable essence holds in my feelings, eye am
at ease moving in this mix-y-uppy place, chaotic beauty

present all around me every day in new york city, quixotic
truths, moral dilemmas arriving as gordian knots, conundrums
deep inside meandering twists & turns map octopus traps filled
with tentacles inside our lives carrying paradoxical images, metaphors
weaving through labyrinthine spiderwebs, crisscrossing intelligence
within moments of dreaming, sweetness, evoke poetry,
as here & now inside the prison cell of this speeding subway car,

then eye see a funky black man swaddled in rags moving slowly
in my direction, now he sits in front of me, leering brown caveman teeth,
he is very, very funky, his smell of decaying flesh wakes me up quickly
from dreaming of poetry surrounded by mangoes, papayas,
the sweetness emanating from thinking of my wife's delectable essence,
my mindset refocuses now on this mad max apparition hovering
in front of me, mirroring the chaotic random beauty suddenly

anywhere you might be in new york city, errançities mix-y-upping
in space with restless, wandering impulses—like my mind deriving information

from everywhere, from within itself—eye focus in on this man facing me now
blooming with rot as he drops his pants, exposes his shriveled private parts,
suddenly eye lose control of my hard-won discipline, blow a gasket,
leap up like a panther, confront him, he flinches, pulls up his pants, begs off,
trembling, obsequious now, his eyes pleading drop from mine,

eye tell him to get off the train at the next stop, he gets up shuffling,
dragging the shadow of a decayed spirit behind him he moves toward the door,
leaving me a blooming odor of a fly-blanketed garbage dump, eye yo-yo back
to the moment before his shock almost froze my liquid creativity, questioned
my fluidity in this chaotic alternate state of the big apple, eye do not know why,
or understand what brought this shadow to slouch as an apparition across from me
a moment ago, though eye do know the mysterious truth of language failed

him—as it has for so many—did not grant him space to move with freedom
into an embracing home amongst the breathing who truly coexist here, dream
of the possibility of this place as a space to reside in inside the chaotic beauty
that is new york city's errançities, where restless love is everywhere present,
found in innovative music created within evolving forms of communication
we recognize as speech, stirred up by mix-y-uppy sounds of poetry, cooked
as linguistic cuisines, simmered down inside pots of our poetic tongues

& dished out as creole, jambalaya, metisisse, mélange, as in a marriage
of divergence, as when a meeting of eyeballs glancing off each other fail to hold
meaning as gesture, though offer intuitive hints of bonding with what we do
not know—have never reached out to know—in this clashing culture of values,
when words embedded inside the same tongues hold love, fraternity, liberty,
brotherhood, but are not recognized as equivalent for this kaput man
who dragged the shadow of his ruined spirit after him when he left the train

What Some Old Men Keep Telling Me

it's all so bewildering growing achingly older, some old men keep
telling me when you become seventy suddenly you wake up
& can't even pee straight, find yourself slow dripping
urine down the front of your pants & you don't even know it!—
it's so embarrassing they say until you catch a whiff of that acrid smell—
assaulting your nostrils—they say the next time you will sit your ass
down on the toilet seat & urinate like a woman,
then there's that thing about climbing up steep stairs—
or going down them straight-legged, like a man walking on stilts,
the frazzled muscles of your legs bunch up,
lodge a protest in your brain in the form of muscle spasms—
charley horses—then aching knees buckle & bitch,
suggest the possibility of collapsing
after you've climbed to the fifth floor with two more to go—
they seem to be telling your brain: "are you kidding me, or what,
you gone mad, or are you stupid, or all three things at once
doing all this strenuous shit, don't you know about heart attacks
coming in a spasm after you've passed sixty-five,"
then there's the looming problem of lost memory stalking you,
especially when you meet people who know your face
but for the life of you you can't remember who they are—
it's almost like some wire tips connecting all the essential memory
links in your brain have suddenly burnt out, especially the ones
connecting names to faces, now you even forget titles
of books you intended to buy when you visit bookstores,
so you will have to start writing everything down
just as that character did in one hundred years of solitude,

sometimes you even call your oldest son your youngest son's name,
just like your ninety-four-year-old mother does with you & your brother
now—remember how you used to laugh at her when she did this—

than there's that fixation about whether or not to use hair dye
every other week to cover up the advancing gray turning your hair
deep white down in the roots of your locks, what's next,
rheumatoid-arthritic fingers gnarling up, refusing to work—even now
you're having trouble picking up dimes off counters—
not to mention all those other body aches,
plus that final horror for men, erectile dysfunction,

now you find yourself going to funerals
if you want a busy social life—there were always a lot
but they seem to have tripled these days,

you got to put a stop to all of this by pursuing dreams you still have
burning with passion until everything just short circuits
& the grim reaper comes around & cuts you down
& you go down to the underworld land of bleached white bones
of memory—eye plan to be burnt up myself,
reduced to ashes, sprinkled like seeds somewhere in the world—

this way you can keep having fun, living a meaningful life
so don't worry about the small shit of growing older
because it's all gonna happen to you, embarrass you
as long as you get up each & every morning

A Hard Quick Rainstorm in Manhattan

a hard quick rain creates rivulets in streets of new york city—
manhattan, harlem, to be exact—glazes patinas on wet
slick surfaces suggesting bits of glass embedded in black thorough-
fares when streetlights throw their beams down, they flicker like diamonds
on backs of raging water currents as a fierce march wind whips through
trees snapping off branches, leaves, shattering umbrellas,
leaves them twisted & broken all over harlem streets
like bodies smashed by speeding cars or trucks,
winds whistling fiercely through shallow gullies running along sidewalks,
turns them into a succession of arpeggios—violent rivers now—sweeping,
like a broom all debris away—a shoe, a half-eaten sandwich
found by a beggar (who looks like he could be anyone's hard-luck brother)
& snatched from his hand by a greedy, snaking airstream,
eye see his look of shock as a mangled pack of torn cigarette butts
is ripped from his hand, see his tears as his cardboard shack,
his blankets cartwheel, hightail it like caped apparitions
down these stunned, flooding streets suddenly whipped hard by winds,
now water spins into whirlpools & the beggar has lost everything
after the storm came calling save his shoes—quarter-sized holes
punched through the worn soles—the grimy, disintegrating
scarecrow clothes on his back, a stocking cap covering
his clotted hair, where voracious lice bed down every night,

still, the rain is mercifully warm, spiritual even, it is spring,
a time when God can be blustery, full of kindness,
in the very same moment (but don't tell the beggar this,
he thinks God forsook him in pure vengeance,

left him out here alone to face this wind-fierce,
gizzard-hearted storm) when all seems to have been lost,

but after all these drumrolls of improvised thunderclaps,
rattle-rattle of rain-sticks on snare drums of metal garbage cans,
prancing dance of accents pinging through streets,
flashing down from thunderheads blooming
& booming overhead, bold zigzagging lightning bolts
unzipping these towering black trousers of clouds, unzipping
the night with electrical élan, after all this rigmarole,
all these breathtaking pellets of rain driven like bullets or nails,
fired into the beggar's face—your face, too, if you're out here—
shot from an invisible gun, you hear the sounds of whiplashing
voices speaking in several tongues, dialects settling down,
become an adagio, a gentle alizé, as the wind transforms itself,
becomes a whispering, lilting breeze as the raging
rivers in gullies turn calm, morph into quiet streams

when light comes in the morning everything will have gone back,
become normal, things will be viewed clearly again
in the brightness of a fresh new day, after the storm has passed
you might think of it as a cleansing dream,
you might just see your image frozen there, framed
inside a clean store window, snapped like a self-portrait from long ago,
you dreamed of, recognize it now inside this clean glass—mirror?—
& it's like seeing a twin you never knew you had for the first time,
in this moment everything might become clear again
as you pass this window, after such a fiend-of-a-storm,
everything might look new, beautifully fresh, again,
even smell sweet after such a storm has come & left
you here, within the refreshing light of this reborn day

Sounds of New York City
FROM HARLEM, 116TH & 7TH AVENUE

for Miles Davis

sounds quixotically mix human languages—wolof, french,
patois, african-american-english, spanglish sprinkled
with pure spanish—inside music—salsa, rap, senegalese mbalax—
the rackaderack of jackhammers rattling streets, cracking asphalt,
shaking minds with noise inside skulls wrapped with skin,
black tar where cars zoom over, shoot down chutes of boulevards,
hang abrupt changes of direction—left or right, what does it matter—
then disappear like insistent car horns in times square
through whatever chaos confronts them—the reality of buildings,
very tall structures with orifices swallowing stuff if windows are open,
allows all the quixotic mixes the big apple lives with every moment—dirt,
debris, pieces of conversations sailing in through open windows like pages
of ripped-up newspapers, voices salty with accents, the squeal of rubber wheels—
to enter, commingle with the city's vociferous languages residing here in the air,
slipping & sliding, punctuated by buzzing flies, mosquitoes, yapping wings
of dog tongues, cats yowling, lightning slicing though air over central park,
where birds skree-skree & yerp-yerp, caw-caw over green grass
in summer, the welcoming whoosh of winds serenading through tree leaves,
like eye imagine charlie yardbird parker soloed long ago in minton's
in his love affair with the way music loop-de-looped during april,
when rains come shimmy-shingling down wet pavements whipping soaked
newspapers swim down chutes of streets around broadway, close to times square,
we move inside ourselves when we enter the subway as it screams back uptown,
the rhythm of train wheels riding the tracks, laying down the syncopation

underlying the rhythm sluicing through this poem, double-backs,
trumpets, bass clarinets & saxophones ride over clicking licks of steel wheels,
reminds me of lenny white, jack dejohnette pulsating on *bitches brew,* gumbo,
screeching sounds, when miles ran the voodoo down, the prince of darkness
stabbing his trumpet breath into a jimi hendrix guitar solo, like a bluesman,
a cat mewing in the dark at a full moon *on the corner,* like muddy waters,
howling wolf—through all this chaos of sound all around us in this place,
so beautifully vital, so creatively imagined in this city of magic
& mystery full of gargantuan appetites & tastes, art congregating
in spaces we pass through every moment, every day, uptown, wherever
we move through this mesmerizing place all others try measuring up to,
this galvanizing metropolis many imitate—its beehive overdrive,
its quixotic mix of skree-skree, caw-caw, music, languages—
whatever the human cost the energy here is always at a boiling point
& those who live here recognize the blowback of this scintillating chaos,
music slipping through cracks to surround you like nirvana & you
love it, deal with it—if you plan to stay here—just keep "gettin up
on the one," every day, miles used to say—just keep "gettin up
on the one," on the one, just keep "gettin up on the one"

2002 Manhattan Snapshot: The War on Terror

two overweight white policemen set up
a roadblock, at 95th and Amsterdam
in new york city, on a cold, windy, november
morning, cars backed up for blocks blare horns
stuck in their anger, my cabby told me
it was money spent on the war on terror, eye thought
did they really think osama bin ladin, or saddam hussein
would be caught dead, or alive in a car in manhattan,
maybe they thought they'd catch some other
kind of terrorist riding in a van,
as if they would come this way since everyone
& their mama knew the roadblock was there,
especially since these men in blue,
their bellies bulging like necks of croaking frogs
strained buttons of their coats as they walked up
slowly to check the long line of cars or vans,
but any terrorists worth their weight in fear,
paying any attention would have been long gone,
so what is this farcical drama all about, eye asked,
my cabby said it was high-ups in government
just letting us know the transfer of tax dollars
they took from us was working to keep wool
pulled way down over our eyes, to keep us blind

A Few Questions Posed

every sunday morning for many years now white people
from all around the globe have flocked in droves
to the first corinthian baptist church, across from where eye live
on 116th street & adam clayton powell jr. boulevard, in harlem
where they stand in long snaking lines sweating bullets in hot,
humid, summer sundays, dressed in un-hip clothing—a few even show
in shorts—shivering, locked in ice-cube winter, dressed like eskimos—
camera-strapped tourists carrying maps of the neighborhood,

they flock up here to hear & see black people decked to the nines,
listen to glory-bird eating preachers deliver holy scriptures,
choirs belting out bring-the-house-down rhythmic glory-be-to-god
rocking gospels, sung in voices so alive you can hear & see angels
strutting the black experience of joy & suffering with wings-
flapping head-nodding blues—though you can't hear real blues up in here
in first corinthian, that would get in the way of the lawd's holy gospel,
the black & white-washed christian message of a blood-drenched legacy
so foreign, it must be made acceptable to these white listeners
with their beaming earnest unquestioning leave-it-to-beaver apple-pie faces,
who keep coming up here full of unreachable complexes,
mysterious maladies, impulses, perhaps thinking their convoluted conundrums
will somehow be fixed, healed, absorbing these holy ghost miracles
sung by aretha franklin clones, like many thought when they voted
for barack hussein obama to be president he would fix everything bush
fucked up, simply because he was a brilliant black man—though none of this
glory has ever seemed to have helped even the most regular

black devotee-clones listening here at first corinthian—even though
many old-timers have been drinking this same holy ghost kool-
aid for decades now, fanning away their heartbreak every sunday

which begs the question why do these white people keep coming
up to harlem to listen to something so far outside their own tradition,
what would happen if the tables were turned
& black people flocked in droves into their neighborhoods on sundays,
would they suffer us, give us directions as we have them
with the same grace, would they welcome droves of christian
others flocking to churches in their neighborhoods,
as native americans welcomed them way back in the day
when they first arrived on these shores from whatever country they fled from,
would they remember all these years they came up to harlem
by subway, taxis, on foot, in cars in large rented buses
taking up all our parking spaces every sunday morning,

would they remember the sermons, the gospel music
they *said* changed their hearts, their spirits, would they/can they change
their dna of privilege, of never ever fully embracing the *other*

Foggy Morning in Port Townsend

heavy fog blooms in the strait of juan de fuca
like tear gas did in boot camp back in fort
leonard wood, missouri, when we practiced fighting wars
& O how the years have run away quick as cats darting through
the dark, to enter this boggy morning of almost silver
rinsed shadows, of trees standing still as silhouette cutouts
outside my windows, on my next to last daybreak here
in port townsend, in another fort
called worden, so still, so quiet here now, where
eye am listening to the music of mozart bloom
from speakers of my laptop computer's cd player,

& O where has all the time run to, wolfgang amadeus,
from your time to here, when we can write & play music simultaneously,
without missing a beat through a technological wizard like this laptop,
what would you think of this invention, old maestro,
you who died so young, like so many musical geniuses,
at thirty-four, crazy as charlie yardbird parker, who went bloated,
drunk to the other side, full of "smack," around the same age as you,
amadeus, have you met him there yet, O great maestro,
have you talked together about how all great music is the same,
have you introduced yourself to miles davis, duke ellington, louis
armstrong, john coltrane, all of whom loved your music,

have you seen them clean in their white bone suits,
polished clean as yours, mozart?

O where have all the years run quick as cats darting through the dark,

to find your music rising here, on a foggy morning rinsed silver?
did you know we would still be listening to your music,
that it would be as familiar as this billowing fog, now lifting,
would be as familiar as memories of tear gas & war on boggy mornings,
trees still standing as silhouette cutouts, shadows of ghost trees
greening up, as the fog lifts to reveal wonders of a new day,

did you know, great maestro, we would still be listening,
as the future will be listening to duke, bird, miles, louis & coltrane,

did you know old great maestro, did you know?

after the fog lifts the day will shine golden green here,
three deer will have already come down out of the woods,
come up to my window, their round luminous eyes wide open,
their wet, soft noses pressed against my window,

listening to your music right now, frozen, seemingly in wonder

did you know old great maestro, did you know?

The Allusion of Seduction

even when you sat in the glowing embers
during that day as any other, the sun
sinking quickly as the breath of a dying man,
who felt the light dimming in his sunken eyes, lingered,
just for a moment, you remembered the soft touch
of a woman's sweet lips you loved
like a cool breeze on your flesh & you lingered
after she left, her perfume hanging in the air there
like seduction, you remembered her incredible tongue
licking so softly, so feathery-light across your keening body,
it was so electric then, is so electric now in your memory,
as this moment is electric when you feel
the beauty of language growing inside a poem,
inside the music of its reference,

on the other hand it is a different moment now
under this black sky filled with stars silent as people
walking around down here imitating zombies,
where you sit, sifting through the wreckage of memory
you hear voices swelling from somewhere deep within
hidden crevices of an invisible stillness, perhaps inside
history, now a plunging hush when once there was a clamoring,
a nervous cacophony filled with agitation, was marching
people around the globe speaking in one voice,
waving banners, thrusting fists—of all colors—
into the glowing air like pistons, then the light suddenly dropped

over the edge of the world during a sunset you remember, when
the police surged forward wearing gas masks,
looking like darth vaders swinging steel batons,
cracking human skulls as if they were piñatas

& hidden behind their sparta shields made people dance
when they shot them with voluble waterhoses
in the glowing light dropping over the edge of the world
at sunset, in this moment here, this eerie silence,
the presence comes rushing at you with garrulous urgency,
drowning out all nostalgia,

& you think of guantanamo, guatanamo, O the shame,
of guantanamo, abu ghraib, the silence,
the creeping national silence of voices ignoring the known,
the cold-blooded depravity, the insulation of ignorance, the silence
we freeze into so we won't recognize the horror
in front of us, the silent drones hovering,
slaughtering over afghanistan, pakistan, it's all so familiar now
as apple pie, the graphic scenes of a tarantino movie,
the impoverishment of spirit we find located
inside ourselves, we have no language that speaks of it

& yet you remember still the sweetness of her lips
brushing over your flesh like feathers of a bird's wing,
her incredible licking tongue lathering
your body with its honey, its seduction of your keening memory
made so electric by her touch, her wondrous perfume
hanging in the air like beautiful language inside a poem
& you linger over the remembrance of all of this,
feel hope is still there, as long as there is love

Searching for a Word

for Margaret

eye am searching for a word
skipping around inside my head
it darts into corners escaping
each time eye reach for it it moves
beyond the length of my tongue
my lips forming the shape of the sound
where the word lives inside one sound
a single syllabic movement
pushes my tongue up & down
inside my mouth becomes almost a clucking
sound when the word begins birthing
forming a singular movement
it becomes familiar as it shapes
itself into a living word
coming back closer to me now
the sound growing out of its womb
easing out of my open pursed lips
as if about to kiss her
comes the sensuous word *love*

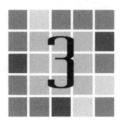

Praise Song for Sekou

for Sekou Sundiata, August 22, 1948–July 18, 2007

it stormed thunder & lightning the day you passed, sekou,
a sky carrying heavy sadness hung down over new york city—
it reminded me of drooping bags under mourners' eyes
after hours of deep, sleepless despair & weeping,
huge eggplant tears dropped from gloomy clouds for you, sekou,
drenched the daytime boppers, flooded the hot, screaming thoroughfares,
right before a steam pipe exploded on 41st street near lexington avenue,
blowing a boiling gray cloud of debris through a gaping, sweltering hole
& swallowing whole a screaming black man alive,
roasting him inside his truck
after burning his clothes off his cooked body,
sending him pleading for help & mercy from horrified, cringing onlookers,
who turned their backs, except for one white man,
who wrapped him in his expensive suit jacket, took him to the hospital,
saved his life on the day you went raging to the other side, sekou,
you threw thunderbolts of lightning into the sky as you went, so angry you were,
we watched them unzip the mood of the day,
watched them zigzag through an onyx sky deep black
as the shining coal of your skin, my luminous friend

& you had so much to live for, so much still to do—
but look at what you *did* do, my brotha, all that beautiful, living
stuff you laid on us full of all those memorable voices on vinyl—
hoodoo priest of sacred magic, singing into this space,

a great dance you were, my friend, a black blues fusing rhapsodic
doobop & jazz, so cool inside your prince-of-light persona
you turned poetry into your own new bop, attitude you had in spades,
a dip in your stride, a knowing look blooming like mystery
inside your been-there-done-that, ever-alert sparkling brown eyes,

you were a walking, breathing barometer of hip, out of miles's tribe,
always at ease inside your skin, your glorious musical language sly & knowing,
a little wink here, a subtle, humorous put-down there, so wise you were, so fly,
always magical, running easy, gliding through who said what to who
& did who do what they said they would do, did they believe in magic, mystery,
when who said they believed in voodoo, then flew, but you knew why
they flew, did what they always do when they are turned around
by directives & go the other way, sekou, you knew why they did it,

knew why they went in the wrong direction to get to where
they *said* they wanted to go, knew why *they* went in the wrong direction
because of their deep conviction they thought they knew the *true* way,
never mind the fact they had never been there before,
but you knew, sekou, so you just flashed a knowing smile when they got lost,
called you back time again for the *right* directions, you just gave up easy
laughter, shook your head, 'cause you knew, sekou, you knew
they didn't like dancing with some meanings under certain words,
like following orders, 'cause you knew they knew the history of the blues,
which meant following some commands might leave a black man in deep,
deep doodoo, confused, because of the history of being black in America
but you loved them anyway, because you knew
some of these people, who sometimes wore suits two sizes too small,
with high-water pants showing tops of white socks everywhere they went,
buttons straining, seeming about to pop off—though they never did—
from the front of their suit coats, 'cause they thought it looked hip, avant-garde,

like ornette coleman, who wore bright red clothes when told to wear all black,
who took strolls in the park when asked to watch someone's house
& left the front door wide open, then scratched their heads, looked puzzled
when they got back, found all the stuff in the house had just upped & left,
who read twenty-page poems at readings of fifty long-winded poets
when told they had no more than one minute to do their thing,

you knew why they always did it like this, sekou, you knew,

so we celebrate you in all your who-went-your-own-way voodoo,
talkin about who copped the sweet bop of all the hipness inside the language,
who hung out with mystery needing to put magic inside your music,
so musicians could take their imagination over the top,

so, solo, sekou, hello, we gonna miss you brotha, your sweet
daybreak-wide smile, though we know you still doin the holy bop
wherever your deep magical spirit took you, sekou,

wherever your deep, hip music flew, we will always hear
your music, your solo, sekou, always saying, hello, hello,

solo, solo with your sweet musical, poetic tongue,
with your deep, humming mysterious voice, that was song

Taps for Freddie

for Miles Davis, Freddie Webster, and Randy Weston, who told me the story

when freddie webster died after shooting poison called "white girl"
through his body/veins, that burned like fire back in chi-town,
in 1947, he thought he was mainlining top-of-the-shelf heroin
but it was strychnine,

                                          maybe battery acid—
bad shit, meant instead for his good friend, saxophonist sonny stitt,
who was beating everybody & their mama out they money
he came in contact with
to satisfy his own big-time junkie habit,
freddie was a junkie too, though he wasn't marked for death
like sonny was—though sonny didn't know he was either
when he passed on the "white death" to freddie as a gift,

freddie's death hit everyone in jazz like a lightning bolt, especially
miles davis, who was as close to freddie as a brother,
so when he heard freddie had died he freaked out, became
inconsolable, like so many other players in the jazz, music orbit,

now, sixty-one years later, down in gosier, guadeloupe, at the creole beach hotel,
may 26, 2008, on what would have been miles's eighty-second birthday—
he's dead, now, too, since september 28th, 1991—
sitting out on the veranda, looking at the sea—the great jazz pianist
randy weston tells me the story of how he, max roach
& the "prince of darkness"—miles davis—went out to coney island beach
to celebrate, remember the short life of their friend, freddie webster,

& miles (a junkie, too, back then, like so many others
during those dark, bright days of music & death in the time of bebop,
during the reign of the biggest junkie of them all,
charlie "yardbird" parker, whose example many were following),
started walking to the edge of the beach, carrying his trumpet
in a brown paper bag—he had pawned his trumpet case
for money, to satisfy his "white girl" habit—

randy said miles walked slowly, deep in thought, head down,
walked toward the sea, kicking up sand as he went,
then he pulled out his golden horn, pointing the trumpet bell east
toward africa, where he said freddie's spirit was now resting,

blew a mournful taps for freddie—who played a mean trumpet, too—
as the atlantic ocean foamed in waves of dying bubbles,

like they bubbled from freddie's mouth the moment he died

Miles's Last Tune Live, August 25th, 1991

when you listen to miles davis live on "Hannibal,"
on his album, *Live Around the World,*
at the hollywood bowl, you hear a memorable solo
performed in a voice emanating from a unreconstructed leader
cracking notes, sliding through changes elusive as hot
mercury, breath slipping out of his horn as quicksilver nuance,
perhaps he knew he was going to the other side soon
not long from that smoggy summer moment,

perhaps though because it was his final performance live
he knew, felt all his extraordinary gifts bleeding out
from his once indomitable, mysterious spirit as if they were
running water whirlpooling down the drain of a kitchen sink,
he seemed too know the end was near—just a little over
a month away—because his playing hinted at this
in a very spooky, haunting way, even though
he wasn't ready to go just yet, had so much more still to do
in his own calculations swirling around inside
his restless, edgy mind embracing errançities,

but death don't wait for no one—not even pure genius—
it just comes when it's time to pay its final visit
like a stealthy thief, whenever

it chooses to snatch away someone's last precious gift of breath,
but miles could go away thankful, knowing he had given

so much enduring, magical artistry,
had left so much beauty to enrich all our lives
left so much great music to remember him by

A Poem of Return: Circa 2008

I.
there is something sounding like the ringing of bells
when you arrive, its music clear in your heart,
you feel the cleansing beauty of its wondrous tone rinsing
through your weary body, carrying rivers of memories,
sweeping over the familiar landscape
until you come to the beloved place, the small house
where so many moments are cascading waterfalls,
moments shimmeringly green as guadeloupian mango trees
are green after clouds drop buckets of rain, after the sun rises
bright clearing the darkness with its brooms
of gigantic, mystical beams of light flashing radiant
& you are there once again inside your head
where everything seems serene, in its place,

memories are seductive things, beckoning you back
to the young women you knew—as you grow older,
their firm, lissome bodies ripple with perfection in memory,
evoke volcanic desires—as you wake up next to
your wonderful sleeping wife holding your body firm,
her tenderness a bell ringing beautiful as any
you have ever heard, a waterfall of spirits
cascading through serenading songs of wind chimes
reminds you of a very deep space that always springs alive
in her, gripping from the very first moment you kissed her
so many moons ago, she still holds you there,

even now, in her warm, magical place of voodoo,
her deep suction pool of sweet love,
even while she is sleeping

2.
there are moments within moments
when you find yourself feeling at home,
as in a smiling face of a stranger walking a road
in st. felix, guadeloupe, on the boulevard st. michel,
in paris, where you see an old black man beautifully dressed
in white linen, a red boutonniere in his buttonhole,
starched white shirt, red tie, a gold tooth flashing like a razor
in the front of his mouth, underneath a wire moustache,
sporting snappy two-toned shoes, a bowler hat & a silver cane
counting off the beat of his hip stroll, two sleek,
beautiful women strutting besides him, arm in arm,
dressed to the nines, their four pointy breasts are invitations
like the stiletto nipples of the women in wilfredo lam's
surreal drawings and powerful paintings,

the three of them seductive, remind me of brash men & women
eye saw way back in childhood, in st. louis, missouri,
in the good-old heydays of the 40s & 50s,
when the riviera & peacock alley were jumping
clubs, in high gear, with wondrously hypnotic people
high-stepping it through galvanizing, innovative music
pulsating clean to the bone of rhythms,
when everything about being hip then was about style & timing,
the promise of new days emanating—
silver breaking from everyone's eyes bright
as scales of fish glinting sparks when sunlight,

or moonlight glances off its back as it swam
close to the surface of the mississippi river,
before the stainless steel arch rose like an indian bow
bent to its limit, ready to send an invisible arrow
flying true into the heart of america's tortured soul,

eye hear crows caw-cawing now in the gray, fetid air
blanketing the river's slow crawl through muddy slime, see
pollution in the form of oil slicks snaking toward the choking
mouth at the gulf of mexico, where future katrinas are
waiting to scream ashore in the soon-coming future,
unleashing howling banshee winds & boiling water beyond
anything—even the most cynical—had ever imagined,
thirty-seven years after john f. kennedy came preaching
the fresh, visionary good news at his inaugural, evoking
dreams seemingly on the verge of really happening,
before assassinations swept the giddiness away—
john f's brains blown out in a motorcade in dallas,
on a cold november day, five years before martin was gone
like a wilted flower in memphis, two years before malcolm
was snuffed out in new york city, five years before
robert kennedy in los angeles, california,
too many others to mention here—before vultures
flopped down slowly from blue notes of storms
weeping all over schizophrenic america—
land of the troubled mocking the millions un-free

still, great american music inspired many of us with obama
to move forward, into a new moment with gusto,
we heard again the genius melodies, memorable as moonwalks
sashaying through the air in the strut of barack's language

so original it began to spread like a great vintage wine,
everywhere you could hear its intoxicating rhythms,
its matchless vigor, its miles davis élan, its coolness, thought

the nation had entered a new age, but we were wrong

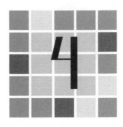

Michael Jackson & the Arc of Love

AUGUST 29, 1958–JUNE 25, 2009

"He was a very fragile soul in a very cruel world"

—DEEPAK CHOPRA SPEAKING ABOUT MICHAEL JACKSON AFTER HIS DEATH ON
  THE MORNING JOE SHOW, JUNE 29TH, 2009

I.

it was always about love from the moment you heard music michael
love of hypnotic rhythm sound when it embraced your heart
penetrated your spirit with a deep worshipping feeling love echoed sweetly
seductive throughout your being with a resonance devoting you to the beat
jumping out of jukeboxes, radios long-playing records singles voices
witch doctors speaking to you in tongues became your hoodoo clan
heroes pulling you into their orbits weaving glorious love
the air pulsating there with magical signature breaths

you heard all this enchantment before you were five in gary indiana
listening to your older brothers sing in a group sucked you into the magic
your sweet-singing mother katherine your cold-blooded gizzard-hearted
father joe abusing you all with bare-knuckle beatings
razor strops whipping you & your brothers into line hard
with constant rehearsals—joe pushed everyone with ambitions of glory
he could not reach as a part-time guitar player with a house full of stair-step
children he had to bring the bacon home to working as a crane
operator—though if truth be told joe thought his rigorous rehearsals/
beatings were necessary acts of sweet love training y'all to deal with
the treacherous people up ahead you boys had to face down the road

you were a musical prodigy michael—a sponge soaking up everything
you recognized innovation from jump—james brown fred astaire jackie
wilson charlie chaplin sammy davis jr. diana ross stevie wonder elvis presley
smokey robinson frank sinatra were your mentors—you learned firsthand
the complexities of love you picked up in your own house wanting to please
with your genius you blew by your older brothers by the age of five
so into entertaining you never had a real childhood so busy you were
rehearsing you got so good so fast you became lead singer of the jackson five
rocketing everyone with you to fame (your little sister janet watching
in the corner of the family nest absorbing like you
& who later would zoom to challenge even you hooking her own
copycat power act of you to your dazzling shooting star/nova)

from the beginning there was no question your coming was a gift
a changing-of-the-guard in pop music merging the complex syncopated
beats of james brown to the holy ghost spirit of your own magical pulse
so genius it soon brought the house down with a new funk hypnotizing everyone
to dance & move you left your four siblings in the dust
because your singular musical juju required you go your own way
without your blood brothers you flew so high with off the wall thriller bad
we are the world dangerous man in the mirror memorable MTV videos
shocked everyone with your breathtaking élan extraordinary to the point
millions were amazed listening to you watching you work your high-wire act
of vocal pyrotechnics coupled with gymnastic "hip-jabbing" dance steps
grabbing your crotch you pirouetted singing billie jean a sequined white glove
slanted like a snake's head high above your head cocked your lithe body
at an angle live on TV we watched you create your iconic moonwalk
your silhouetted razor-sharp cutout image of black & white fingers saluting
your hip-slanting black fedora hat in a memorable pose we can't forget

your dominance was complete after *those* mind-blowing images
showed off your unparalleled hoodoo stamping your image into the air
on stage your conjurer presence imprinted there in our memory
mysterious as a sculptural magician—you carved out your space lived in it
practicing a kind of musical cartomancy melody still your seductive secret—
you had no need though to pronounce words correctly in songs
you had poetic license to create neologisms spontaneous magic on the spot
you improvised modalities you were a beautiful geegaw we all looked at fascinated
until the shine began to wear off your bobble when you broke your nose in 1979
then your hair caught fire in 1984 filming a pepsi commercial
flames left the top of your head burnt bald as a cue ball consigned you to wear
that weird-looking long halloween black witch's wig in public forever
after that your facial changes began—by 1986 your face was transformed
changing the beautiful geegaw we all knew & loved into something strange—
after all these tragedies your bubble finally began to burst

first you were over-loved then totally misunderstood after your flower
bloomed into something beyond comprehension for so many
who knew nothing of the deep pain you were going through every day
trying to find love—as your power turned special your image was ubiquitous
everywhere suddenly you were no longer the cute little black genius geegaw
boy you had suddenly morphed into a creepy man-child
metamorphosing before our eyes you looked so otherworldly
wearing the long black witch's wig no matter it covered your scarred head—
who knew why it was there the plastic surgery bleaching your skin from encroaching
vitiligo those images of you carrying bubbles the chimpanzee around
buying bones of the elephant man sleeping in that polio-looking oxygen chamber—
you began to seem so out of step with everyone
divorced from even those who still loved you & your music

when you outbid paul mccartney for the beatles music catalogue
everything began going wrong for "wheat" folk/critics—
they started hating you—after all you were still just a little black boy to them
they thought you were getting too big for your britches making boatloads of money—
no matter your genius worldwide celebrity your hope to love everyone—
for you what the world always needed was "love sweet love"
but few knew how to get there then or now or whenever
because love is a deep life-changing thing hard anytime maybe
impossible for many though it still is the answer if truth be told

all this malice caught you by surprise since you were an innocent—
though sharp as a razor when it came to business—who only wanted love
to please everyone with your art for everyone to love you too
the heart of your music taking wings in rhythm striking love
like lightning zigzagging your iconic beats across a menacing black sky

2.
suddenly you became a piñata in the 24/7 corporate media world
for anyone to swing at in public because of problems they thought
you had—sleepovers with macauley culkin emmanuel lewis at neverland— then
tom sneddon the santa barbara sheriff wanted to look for vitiligo on your penis
drove the bogus 1993 child molestation charges
though many knew the charges were made up by greedy parents—
then you married lisa marie presley divorced her married weird debbie rowe
had two children by her before you divorced odd debbie too spoke on that strange
martin bashir—now an msnbc anchor—documentary showing you buying that gaudy
expensive junk then you dangled your son prince from a berlin balcony
went through that bogus 2005 trial before being exonerated though
your spiritual image in the media was in total tatters after that

dealing with you became a bolus stuck in many people's throats—
it wasn't about the music we all loved but about you michael—

your strangeness dominated was fed intravenously to your critics
like the prescription drugs you were taking now as lupus came down on you
vitiligo changed the way you looked as white spots spread like a plague
over your brown body forced you to bleach yourself all white if you still wanted
to entertain in public & you did because entertaining was in your blood
was what you always needed to do to be whole—but few wanted to see
your spots on stage the cartography of your skin—when you let us view it
not covered with clothing—hands face neck slivers of arms wrists
fingers/tips palms your lips turned all red now with fresh lipstick though
the most bizarre change in your face was your newly reconstructed nose
looking as though it had been assaulted in war showing all those battle scars
no plastic surgeon could conceal—the grotesque changes—
when scrutinizing cameras zoomed in you couldn't hide the damage
no matter how much money you spent it couldn't hide the bizarre transformation
of your face with any kind of makeup—for this there was no grace,

all this bizarre renovation took a toll on you—& us—dominated the media
instead of your music your deep abiding seductive spiritual love—
this was the tragedy of your long fall from grace michael this new definition
fixed you in the media—racist as it always is for black people—
with snippets of facts false truths innuendo—though in the end your love
& your music will be your timeless gift to us all not some prying camera news-
        reader/voiceover who never wanted to know the real you

but at the end you were a little boy isolated in a fifty-year-old body
deep sadness in your once beautiful round lightbulb eyes
though you were ready to bask in the spotlight onstage once again
with your "this is it" london concerts to show everyone you still had it
the incredible seductive magic to amaze but death—a kind of weird suicide
when you rolled the dice for seven it came up snake-eyes—ending it all
pulled us into profound grief mourning left us pondering the question—
what would have happened had you not left way too soon

3.

death found you after midnight when you finished rehearsing your new show
from the staples center you went home happy that last night
because you had once again entered the wondrous zone of your artistic genius
you were trying to sleep when you checked yourself out with an iv
drip dripping the deadly anesthetic propofol—you called it your "milk"—
drip dripping death into your collapsed starving veins needle marks tracking up
& down your paper-thin white arms your skin almost translucent
when you entered "the valley of death" you had long spoken of—
you went there skin & bones bald as a bowling ball save a little peach fuzz
on top of your head under the long witch's wig (did you wear it to bed at night
michael trying to fall asleep through terrible insomnia) drugs running
like polluted rivers through your ghostly anorexic body
swallowed by tents of your clothing—in the end you were still
responsible for your own life michael the way you lived it with yes-people
surrounding around you giving you everything you wanted—not needed—
responsible for your own death if you killed yourself as eye think you did—
depressed as you were at the end though happy too with great joy
for your comeback tour surrounded by your children & music

when you took your spirit to the other side of the veil you went
free of the pain around you since childhood the savage scrutiny relentless
prying eyes of media cameras searching for anything they could find—
still you were responsible for yourself michael for your children
all those who loved you but you wanted all of it—the fame you craved
the spotlight shining on you with vengeance—did you forget the baggage
that comes with being a nova/star—& it finally trapped you
your beautiful spirit inside a spiderweb of your own making—
didn't you see the poisonous media spider of death coming for you—
in the end you didn't deserve the terrible hatred & envy that came your way
but you surrounded yourself with all those vampire vultures & that deadly
spider fed off you greedily until you were a shell of skin & bones

some say you had duffel bags packed with cash hidden in the mansion
when you died—there was news someone in your family bum-rushed your death
scene trying to take that money—perhaps it was only rumor like so much else
swirling around your life until it became a kind of truth—whatever it was
the spectacle surrounding your death was heartbreakingly sad
revealed just how important you were to making money for others—no matter
death—like elvis—your porcelain-white flesh soon will become memory
but your music & artistic élan will live pulsating magic & love
transformative as anything eye have ever heard or seen in my life

the announcement of your death was like a gigantic broom
sweeping everything off front pages of newspapers—
across the globe your death totally dominated airwaves
people wept danced celebrated your life played your songs once again—
your funeral was something to behold you laying there unseen
inside your flower-draped golden coffin as friends & family testified
honored your name your music your arc of human love

up over staples center—kobie bryant's mecca—the shape of a heart appeared
above in the blue sky—inside berry gordy spoke sage words about you
al sharpton gave a powerful speech a gospel choir sang poignantly
so did usher & stevie wonder pulsating images of you dancing singing electric
graced a screen in all your glory brooke shields spoke incisive words
evoked humor a deep personal friendship then your daughter paris
broke down weeping at the end of the ceremony
told everyone how much she loved you would miss you greatly
this brought everyone to tears in this moment of mourning you michael—though
we also wept for paris her loss—when the ceremony was over the final image
a single spotlight shining on a lone microphone standing center stage
was an homage to you as your poignant voice sang for us
to look at ourselves finally "& make a change"

CODA

jagged lightning rips open a black stormy sky over new york city
on a day late in july over a month since you went to "the valley of death"
the lightning tearing the mood asunder reminds me of you hip-jabbing
your signature fractured cutout silhouette dance jagged
white against black evoking whatever beauty comes to mind during an act
of creative power as lightning strikes bring with it a bold sense of fiery
resurrection of savage beauty the unbridled creative power of music
perhaps sudden lightning & thunder is a reminder of demons possessing us all—
especially you michael despite your gentle spirit—perhaps the sudden fierce
lightning eye saw today is like you—no iambic hexameter line could contain
your combustible zapping spirit no broken-up space-filled stanzas
all over the page could reflect the arc of your hauting voice aching with longing
though sometimes bright with hard steel glittering off the arch rising above
the mississippi fronting downtown st. louis during clear nights or days
when the moon or sunrays dance across the glittering surface curved
like a bow in the hands of one of our native american indian ancestors
your compact diamond-hard lightning-quick energy zeroing in during a moment
focused in rhythm inside the music dance your imaginative quicksilver grooves
within your electric spirit hovering in the sky lancing lightning music
with thunder thrilling with fierce beauty keening through
the firmament of our memory with a discharge of incredible energy

your iconic image there in skies around the globe reminds us
of your glory your creativity magic imagined with love teaching us
honing in on mystery & beauty—you will always be there michael
as spirit a sudden bolt of lightning ripping open the sky like today
your arc of music beckoning us to always "make a change"

Thoughts on a Sunday Morning in Goyave

for my son, Porter, on his 24th birthday

it is sunday morning, 5:30 A.M. when the roosters began crowing
throughout my goyave neighborhood, their *cockadoodledoos*
reverberate up & down hills of this valley
in their age-old struggle to be the first to announce the rising of the sun
from its grave in the night sky—somewhere in the east, the morning breaks through
cotton-candy gray clouds cruising over a tranquil caribbean sea, mirrors
the sadness of the earth below, where strutting, preening roosters
remind me of puffed-up politicians crowing their bogus pretense at sagacity,
peddling machiavellian snake-oil schemes of compassionate hope
to neutered flocks of sheep making beelines for edges of cliffs—
it's an age-old maneuver/scheme to sacrifice the poor
in overcrowded populations—
now my thoughts spin north
to the american capital, bumbling dupes of the bush administration—
the gang who can't shoot straight, or keep their ducks in a row—who every day
come spinning complete falsehoods with straight faces in place,

today, throughout this dark, desolate period of our lives
there are so many political hatchet men all over the globe—
the hypocritical lapdogs of england, avaricious hyenas all over africa,
oil-drunk royal pigs of saudi arabia, the slimy, fez-wearing fools
posing in kabul, afghanistan,
the bumbling idiots leading israel & palestine, lizard-eyed weasels
all over the caribbean, mexico, central & south america, paralysis all over
europe, canada, australia, the far east, russia, everywhere, these men—

women too—imitating fat croaking frogs wallowing in cesspools,
surrounded by phantasmagorias of poisonous reptiles
flicking out tongues, eyeing their next prey

what are the root causes of all these age-old disagreements,
these fruitless wars without end, this poverty of spirit, imagination
sacrificed on the bonfires of vanity, greed, power, racism, xenophobia,
these dangerous, self-righteous religious creeds, this exhausting
mindset of white-skinned privilege
as an unconditional birthright to do what they want,
when they want, to anything & everyone on earth

where has the love gone on this grieving, polluted planet,

now my thoughts turn back to these roosters crowing
throughout this beautiful valley,
eye see their need to outdo each other when thrown together
in the same backyard—they argue, fight, but do not kill each other
unless trained by men—as we humans have since time immemorial,

all eye know for certain is that it's sunday, march 25th,
it is beautiful here in goyave, today is the birthday
of my youngest son, porter, twenty-four years old, living out his dream
of becoming a professional basketball player, in romania,
we can only hope he succeeds, that he's well, happy,
hope we've taught him to love, live peacefully with others,
to do the best he can with what he's given, to be thankful
the sun rises each morning, thankful
for the sweet love & good cheer
he brings into our lives every day

& into the sacred lives of so many others

Goyave Night Scene

the roll-up door lifts next to a yellow light bathing
the black & white photo of miles dewey davis
resting on the white wall of our house in goyave
as a cool sea breeze tongues in, massages my face & toes
where eye am stretched out on a black & white couch,
looking at the leonine "prince of darkness" dressed in black
lizard pants, open white shirt, a slender black scarf hangs
from his neck, he is young, handsome, beautiful even,
looks taut as a black panther slouched in repose,
his face looks pensive, lost in thought, he holds his golden
trumpet cocked in the air, as if about to play with the night
sounds of frogs, birds, & crickets syncopating into my house
as they serenade us with their pulsating musical grooves,
outside, imagined ghost-voices emanate from shadows,
tremble through bushes clinging to fences,
eye hear a bat's sharp cry cleave the night like a razor
slicing through flesh, bone, gristle, as a bloodcurdling
scream of a dog hit during rush-hour traffic reminds us
death is always near, right around the corner
& all is not paradise here, though close as anything
eye have ever imagined, close as anything beautiful
can be to the paradox of mystery, surprise, wonder

Sitting on My Veranda, Facing the Caribbean Sea

for Derek

eye sit on my veranda in goyave, listen to voices serenading,
climbing out of foaming waves of the caribbean sea,
hear them suds on shore murmuring of past apocalyptic histories
clashing with truth,
small rocks & sand tickling bare toes of swimmers
lying on beaches here, perhaps provoke in them dreams of strolling
electric streets hip in amber, of lovers holding hands in paris,
new york city—wherever dreams carry them to magic,

it is november here, right before transforming darkness falls
with its bejeweled black cape sweeping over the entire sky with flair,
then a flourish of cicadas & crickets come out raising sound from their legs
rubbing up against each other with passion, they join choirs of frogs
in a symphony swelling the night with orchestral compositions of wonder—
like lyrical casuarinas they fuse with voices of birds whispering
from leaves of trees bowed by wind-tongues until they sing beautifully

with melodies, as traffic music of passing cars climb into my ears
drummed from highway one, mix with spinning rubber tires, wash them
into a whooshing sound of charging engines trailing off into the distance,
where they disappear down the plunging road into the night—
are they going into a quick death of wreckage or a slow aging one?—
a certainty we all have to rendezvous with sooner or later—

eye turn from the echo chamber of my ears & look south
toward st. lucia, where my old friend derek walcott lives in a lovely house,

also facing the caribbean sea & eye hope he is still writing wondrous poems
as he approaches his eightieth birthday in january 2010—
we have known each other almost half our lives now,
since 1968 when eye met him in los angeles—eye first read of trees
called casuarinas in one of his poems & loved the beauty of the word,
the sound lilting with syllables evoking a dance
of the sea washing in

as now, when it is 3:00 A.M. here & the new rooster next door begins
his ritualistic crowing a little early—it is misty now,
whispers of rain are falling, though frogs & crickets are still making music—
soon the day will return, waking us from sleep again & we will perhaps catch
a moment of beauty when we open our windows to the light
spilling its radiance into our rooms fresh with songs of birds, perhaps
the new day will bless me with a gift of an original poem
& fecund ideas to compose many others

A Veil of Transparent Rain

a veil of transparent rain advances toward shore
from the aqua green water carrying a rainbow
extending up top to bottom, swirls of mist
wrap themselves around the dazzling arching colors
as two sailboats enter the miraculous mix
the wind picks up everything, seems so deliciously magical,
mysterious as secrets, when salt water of a pulsating caribbean sea
off the coast of goyave, guadeloupe, changes color from aqua green
to a wet slate gray mirroring fast-moving clouds above,
motoring toward the northwest where the sun is setting

at this moment eye remember a few days before
a french plane fell like a stone from the sky,
dropped into the middle of the atlantic ocean, due east
from where eye now sit—they found two bloated bodies floating
on this day when this poem is coming to life, two days after president obama
delivered his historic speech in cairo, egypt
dealing with the middle east, on the same day he spoke
of d-day in france, one day after celebrating
the jewish holocaust at buchenwald,
a day after mexican children were roasted in a car
somewhere in another preventable tragedy—

out there another preventable disaster of death is lurking
to cause 9/11 fear beyond the uncaring selfish gaze of so many people
greedy beyond measure is what eye am thinking
as this veil of transparent rain advances softly

as luminous green leaves of my mango tree wave *hello hello*
they shimmy dance on tongues of winds over french-tonguing
words, probing, in the distance, caressing in goyave sweet
as murmuring showers sweep in, bringing the beginning of darkness,

now the sun settles down behind blooming mountains in the west,
nightfall inches in as secrets nourishing winds push the clouds
further north, past the looming shadows clearing the sky
for the moon to climb bright into a night sky full of stars—
reminding me of pearls or diamonds plopped down
on the black suede rug in a new york jeweler's shop,

it is magically mysterious & eye ask myself once again
how do these things always happen every day
in this world filled with miracles & horrors—
seemingly coming suddenly as that rainbow a few hours ago—

coming during moments we least expect, bringing surprise,
as now, when stars flash bright in a clear dark sky

A March Day in Goyave

eye look out my window & see waves
rolling in from the caribbean sea,
one foaming whitecap after the other,
they look like spools of salt tongues dissolving
into blue-green pools of water turning brown
beneath a sky full of cruising seahorse clouds
pushed hard by whipping march winds,
so musical they make leaves shake their green bodies
in collective ecstasy—eye watch the sweet dance
of sparkling light wash shimmering over
bouffants of trees dangling mangoes, breadfruit,
while underneath papayas, dazzling alpinia
purpuratas shimmy on their stalks, ladder up
blossoms of flames, as heliconia rostratas,
droop their pelican-head flowers of red
& yellow reminding me of lynched men,
whose heads are akimbo over a taut noose
as they turn slowly in airstreams,
sagging, like billie holiday's strange fruit
flowering on vines, tree branches sagging,

now eye watch the light grow dimmer,
dying as the sun drops over the mountains
due west, where the day is still bright
though growing darker by the ticking second,
as the need felt by those who go to war grows

black as the sky above where they fitfully sleep
& die, now a full moon stares down silently
its milky orb of a blind man, unseeing
though light from its globe probes beams into shadows,
reveals nocturnal creatures scavenging through
dark hours needed by prowling vampires,
though earth's incubating seeds still ripen,
grow when the moon is at its zenith,

eye follow the footsteps tracking now across
the beach's sand, the alluvion—carnivorous tide—
eating its own essence, one foaming wave after another,
soon it will go the way of so many men at war,
dead upon arrival, never knowing what
shot them through the heart was the greed of rich men—
with cravings like themselves—who fancy
almost everything, but who understand so little

A Day in the Life of King Rooster & His Son

eye think the young rooster in our big backyard in goyave
guadeloupe, is practicing his raggedy, hoarse crowing
perhaps to refine it, make it more lyrical,
he starts early every morning, way before daybreak births
light from darkness, before a rising sun cracks through cloud
cover, becomes the golden coin eternally celebrated
fixed as it spins up there in luminous sapphire-blue air,

today the young rooster started crowing at 3:00 A.M., an hour
before others in our bucolic neighborhood
opened their beaks to *cockadoodledoo,* to defend territory,
perhaps also to warn other roosters of imminent danger
(least that's what some esoteric rooster experts write
in their tweedy little books, though others—including me—feel
they might not know what they're talking about—perhaps referencing
some arcane theory hatched in wombs of their heads like eggs,
since roosters don't speak human, & experts don't talk rooster,
how would they know what roosters always crow about)

anyway, poppa king rooster—dad to our early-crowing cock—
is peeved with his youngin today—perhaps he didn't like his son crowing
an hour before *he* did this morning, while perched
high up, where the king always looks down on his kingdom from his throne
hidden amongst thick leaves of a bois carrié tree, right before night leaves,
waiting to crow the first *cockadoodledoo* of the morning
during the mysterious thin window between dark gloom & bright sun,

before daybreak births light from its dark womb, stirring invisible voices,
this king cock rules down here in our backyard—not his son—
sitting on his throne, looking at the sea, he thinks in his rooster head
it's *his* sovereign right to break the first sleep-shattering call,
the first *cockadoodledoo* each & every morning

he is pure royalty around here, you can tell by his great size,
deep-brown lustrous body feathers—light beige around his neck—glorious
red comb, large red wattle hanging under his beak,
jet-black hackle, white spot on top—his rich melodic crowing
is to die for—no other rooster in this area comes close—
plus he struts straight up like nobody's business,
nipping & pecking his brood of plump hens, prancing,
clucking like an alto saxophonist soloing after he comes across something
good to eat, or making sexual passes at his hens—
he's something to behold—eye watch in amazement as he preens,
boasts, swaggers, clucking, then blows his soaring
cockadoodledoo solos,

yet every day his growing son—a little older, bigger than a cockerel
though nowhere near large as his dad, challenges his rule constantly,
encroaching on the king's sovereign territory—two backyards,
side by side—the young cock starts crowing when
he's supposed to be napping, then starts flirting—when
he's not pecking for seeds—with the young frisky hens—not his
mother though—concubines in his father's harem—
this sexual impudence irritates the king no end,
makes his anger rise—add to this his son's incessant off-key crowing
throughout the day—especially today,
after he gave the impudent first call before his dad—all this
has rubbed against the king's last nerve until it's raw,

now he starts chasing his son around & around our yard,
fiercely clucking, nipping at the rascal's small hackle,
telling the little snot to stay in his place, in this, his kingdom,
so they run & swerve & dart like two swirling dervishes,
they destroy our flowerbeds, duck under bramble pretzel bushes,
bleached snapped-off tree branches reminding of sharp bones,
looking like bats-out-of hell they run like roadrunners
at breakneck speed, their combs flat atop their heads,
wattles shaking from side to side under their beaks
thrust out in the air, their skinny pole legs a blur,
they run clucking, swerving around or trampling
every obstacle—it is a sight to behold

& when they're finished, the young cock has been chased—
for the moment—outside the king's royal fiefdom,
to find himself a new yard for the day, to lick his wounds,
his hurt prince's pride, though he & the king know for certain
he will be back again tomorrow
& the ritual will begin again

but today the mighty king beats his chest in victory at the edge
of his kingdom with his short little wings, useless except to flutter
up to branches of the bois carrié tree
& his throne, where he hides, so rats won't eat him,
sleeping through nights, before crowing in daybreak,
now he rears back his head, opens his beak & blows
a triumphant *cockadoodledoo*—
reminding me of a soaring paul robeson solo—
then he struts back through the yard for his hens—& me—to see,
preening, letting us know *he* is the only king here for now, on this day
& his impudent son is only a pretender—

but both know the day will come when the cock
will take his father's throne—pretender no longer—
& the king will be chased away or go into someone's pot for dinner

but today isn't that day, so long live the rooster king of our backyard
in goyave, guadeloupe, long live the rooster king,

the rooster king, the rooster king, long live the king

Short-term Amnesia

for Monsieur Lulu, Mademoiselle Rosa, Bones & Food

in guadeloupe when margaret & eye go to the homes of our friends micheline
& luc to eat, we often take bones to please their two little dogs,

mademoiselle rosa & monsieur lulu—most times when we go, rosa, the oldest,
shaped like a long wiener, snatches the bones from our apprehensive fingers

tout de suite, as a snapping turtle would if it were always hungry as rosa & lulu are,
though lulu holds back, his large round dark eyes searching our eyes for a clue

as to what is about to happen, the inquiry posed in his questioning orbs is do we have
a bone for him or don't we & being dog royalty his point of view doesn't predispose him

to regular bouts of begging, because he kinda don't want to go there, but will if need be
because he is smart enough to know every situation is different, so he plays it

different all the time, but when either gets a bone they disappear until finished, then,
return, their tails—hers short, his long—wagging furiously, their eyes glistening

in anticipation, because they always expect more—they seem to be constantly suffering
short-term amnesia—so they follow the lust of their stomachs, like most humans,

not what might be best like take a break, cool down those desires, those unchecked
cravings our stomachs dictate, though we know in the dog-world, or the human-world,

there is no control of our lusts—please, let's not talk crazy here—soon, both lulu
& rosa are in front of us again, looking up, sad orbs beseeching, inconsolable

when they discover we have no juicy bones left, nor one scrap of food
since dinner hasn't been served yet—they settle into their pattern of begging,

their eyes imploring, though their grief isn't bottomless as it is when we arrive
with nothing to give, which happens sometimes when we come straight

from the airport to the home of our friends after arriving from new york city—
then their sadness is palpable from the start, no interval, or pulse of bliss interrupts

their pleading stares bleeding, mourning, glistening with grief they nail us
with hunger every time we look their way—their sorrow is complete, total,

stays intact until we deliver a scrap of any little thing edible we toss their way,
but we better be quick if we don't want them erupting into a storm of barking—

if we deliver food they might show us a flicker of redemption, perhaps
a slight slow-motion wagging of their tails, though joy is still not in their vexed eyes,

only a slight easing of displeasure, a tiny hint—perhaps, the start of rapprochement—
when they sit upright, backs straight on haunches, his tail beneath him, hers sweeping

the ground in quick flicks like a long-handled brush when someone uses it
to clean up dog mess left on a floor, if they think food is on the way,

ready to drop satisfaction into always-growling stomachs,
then we could be forgiven our sins, but if their desires are not rewarded

they cease all pretense at protocol—good will is definitely out the window—
& they start barking profusely their deep vexation & disappointment now profound

Mad Max

Wrecked cargo ship off the coast of Gosier, Guadeloupe
for Jean Marie & Fabienne

we were sailing on jean marie & fabienne's fishing boat, *calmis,*
while colorful little sailboats cut through waves around us
lapping, foaming with history, & above, cotton-white
clouds cruised through the bright blue sky,
the sun & soft breezes caressed us with seductive love,
when suddenly we saw it rising up ahead—
a rusted skeleton of a cargo ship run aground off the pristine coast of gosier,
so long ago it had become a natural habitat for fish—
barracuda, lobster, dorade, sturgeon—
its brown hull broken into five parts—the jawbone of an ass,
the jutting ribs of a dinosaur, a dilapidated watertower,
a filigreed globe of the world, a broken fence—
looked like those corroded derelict machines in a mad max movie,
its horror rising up like some prehistoric relic,
a monster, dead for centuries, uncovered at last in the roiling
salt waves of the atlantic breaking over its carcass,
foam licking white at the top of the sea's hissing curl,

then the waves swelled from the east on their way northwest
toward goyave—where margaret & eye live—caused the airstreams
to pick up out of the blue, drove the boat into a pelting rain
blocking our view of those wondrous mountains
backdropping our small house, ghost arms of clouds
& mist descended with searching hands crawling down those verdant green

slopes, their long slender fingers probing crevasses in the lush hillsides,
secret nooks that cause my imagination to run wild
with notions of what exotic treasures might be found there
that might equal my discovery, on this blessed day, of the ruined
mad max wreck, rusting off the coast of gosier

Haiti Haiku

nothing like an earth-
quake, to level the playing
field, for rich & poor

Earthquake: Haiti

for Monique Cleska, Patrick Delatour & Daddy George

it struck as always without notice or warning,
struck at 4:53 P.M., January 12, 2010,
the sun was smiling down on countless
people bustling home in rush-hour
port au prince traffic, everywhere crowded streets
pulsated humanity when the earth started shaking violently
for thirty-five seconds it shook, rumbled,
then a yellow-white cloud of dust rose up—
& if you were high up in the mountains looking down
you would have thought perhaps you were above
hurricane storm clouds roiling with fury—

thirty-five seconds the earth was an undulating rollercoaster,
thirty-five seconds devotees called upon Voodoo gods,
                          Christian gods for mercy, forgiveness,
thirty-five seconds of fear wrestled inside frazzled brains,

someone on a balcony filming the scene below said,
"the world is coming to an end," just as wailing rose,
just as the sound of dirt and rock cracked apart
underneath the earth, grinding plates screamed from tension, broke,
one sliding underneath the other, creating fissures up above
as the ground split apart, riven, multiplied into snaking fingers
that couldn't strangle the many voices that rose
from everywhere, unimaginable horror spoke—

the montana hotel where eye wrote half of *Miles:*
The Autobiography with Miles Davis,
collapsed, pancaked floor by floor into a pile
of rubble, killing hundreds as it went down—then pain
exploded through countless brains, skulls, bodies, arms, limbs,
as concrete walls caved in on them

thirty-five seconds seemed like thirty-five slow-moving lifetimes,
thirty-five seconds collapsed edifices of religion, power, privilege,
thirty-five seconds sucked poor people even deeper
down into whirlpools of choking poverty,

the end of the world as haitians knew it came suddenly,
entered their eyes as a revelation,
shocked, that a day so beautiful
could turn so wicked in thirty-five-second blinks of an eye,
thirty-five seconds of violent eruptions (perhaps more heinous than the rule
of savage dictators like papa doc duvalier
who slaughtered tens of thousands like joe gaetjens, the hero
soccer player, who scored the only goal for america when
they beat the english team back in 1950)

thirty-five seconds of shaking madness & death down
on this first day of suffering—before stench of rotting bodies
shocked nostrils & the imagination after a few days—
then on the second day a miracle happened
when homeless people began to sing, chant, dance & pray
under the moonlight and stars

then what eye always knew to be true popped into my mind

that the haitians are a remarkable people,
spiritual, beautiful, creative, strong, resilient—eye knew
they would bounce back from this over time—
they always have in the past, they will do so now—

though this time good news will be a long time coming

Hurricanes

first eye am dreaming of blue skies followed by slight murmurs
resembling lisps of people speaking, trembling through silence
(like lovers whispering in bedrooms or gatherings of friends)
followed by fluffs of small white clouds soft as cotton candy
(they remind me of scouts of an advancing army searching for clues
to take back, information that what is coming behind them is a menace)
still eye am inside my imagination dreaming of the golden eye
of the sun warming my day with its beauty & healing power

but out in space seeking a way to cross warm sea waves tossing
turning down below is a growing cluster of whirling cumulus clouds
gathering around a vortex of swirling air rising up as errançities
hissing with salted white spray starting to speak in tongues
as it coalesces around an engine of wind giving commands now
(the engine that sent the cloud scouts out searching for clues)
to explode upward into angry vapor obliterating its cousins
soft as cotton candy it begins to move forward gaining speed
these new vexed vapors wrap themselves around the vortex—
like whirlpools of shouting hissing political voices disagreeing
throughout congresses all over the world every waking day—
soon some have purple eyes—category fives of evil—
threats to everything around them they will hurl themselves
boiling into our consciousness after acquiring names like hugo
katrina rita dean will raise fear of catastrophic judgment days
as they advance with howling voices of apocalyptic errançities
churning every-which-way full of violent linguistic maelstroms

swirling masses of cumulus advancing over warm sea water
imitating whirlpools spinning into fives massive human militias—
destined to destroy everything they touch when they approach

Lusting after Mangoes

for Margaret

eye get up before the sun imitates a burst of fire,
igniting a huge explosion as light
sweeps all shadows into secret corners everywhere,
it must be—as miles davis once told me—
about timing,
eye must arrive precisely behind

my house in the yard, under the tree full of mangoes,
a split second before the rooster comes leading
his posse of hens, cute little voracious chickadees,

right after the rats have abandoned the eating field—
which is my abundant, sprawling, tropical backyard—
where fresh mangoes fall in season, ripe beyond belief—

like tender breasts—sweeter than a luscious kiss—
succor from someone you love, you must be there on time,
as the prince of darkness told me, to gather that saccharine,

taste those luscious sweet mangoes where they fell
when the sun burst through yawning hours of the dawn sky,
opening it up with its cutting rays as would a can opener

a tin of candy treats you tasted once & everything
seemed new, as when you wake up, find your lover there
breathing softly at your side, succulent as a mango

Searching for Mangoes: Second Take

for Margaret also

it's a race against time in our backyard
in goyave, trying to beat field rats,
ants & chickens to the sweet prizes—
delectable griffy mangoes falling from our two trees—

it's a race against sharp tiny teeth & beaks
penetrating the hard green skins brushed with rose,
yellow blush, once they've nestled on the ground

before the rats take healthy bites, the chickens peck
holes in the skin, the ants stream through the flesh en masse,
wherever they find openings they swarm all over
the sweet nectar flesh,
gobble up all the tissue,
leave behind, over time, dried up
   leather-brown corpses,

they remind me of slain soldiers on a battlefield
littered underneath umbrellas
of our twin trees,
where the rats prowl only at night,
the chickens only during moments of sunlight when it is safe—
they fear attacks from packs of always-hungry rodents—
the ants come whenever they choose
& eye only during hours when the sun is smiling,

it is a race against some odds, too—who knows when
a strong wind will come, blowing through all those
overloaded tree branches, shake loose those sweet mangoes,
send them plunging toward an unwelcoming earth,

so the trick for me is to arrive first at daybreak,
right after the rats have eaten their fill, abandoned the field,
before the chickens come out of their sleep to peck holes—
the ants are always there but need chicken holes
to stream through—just when the new mangoes have plopped
down on the ground, ready for *my* harvest,

it's all about timing
as miles davis once said, who gets there first
enjoys the fruits of their labor,
the sweet golden nectar of a mango's ripe flesh,
succulent, luscious beyond description

Listening to Black Birds

eye listen to a flock of black birds jamboreeing high up
in the large mango tree in my backyard in guadeloupe,
wonder what they are jabbering about hidden
within lengthening shadows of twilight approaching darkness
spreading its wings like these birds when they take flight,

their jabbering reminds me of black people gathered on corners
underneath my window in harlem during summers running down
whatever game their jazzy, jambalaya language offers up
as food for thought—the loud insistent slap of dominoes hitting tables,
spiced with boasts of men—women, too—who have mastered
the sarcastic lingo of tongue-in-cheek put-downs mixed
with salt & pepper wisdom saucing up air around the game,

eye have always loved listening to language like this improvising
solos spit from lips—or beaks when talking about black birds—dripping
syllables popping through firecracker sentences dropping neologic words,
sounds into everyday lexicon of hip oral speech—language
has always been the fuel driving duende/music of my poetry,

but these black birds are a special case since eye can't enter
the meaning of their language—are they happy or mad, hungry
or sad, making fun of humans like me listening to them perplexed,
trying to decipher—translate—their intricate jabbering music
packed with jackhammer rhythms—a language so high-pitched,
so insistent it seems close to frenzy, as if they were discussing
important topics to themselves, relevant to survival of the globe,

perhaps what they are jabbering about is crucial for us, too,
though how would we humans know since few of us listen,
or even hear anything we say to each other
when it comes to important matters
like, for instance, the waging of eternal war
pollution of the planet with oil—what about the gulf of mexico, alaska—
the politics of corruption by outright bribery, runaway, rampant greed—
the list of human deafness goes on & on, dominates the sordid,
sad history throughout the blindness of the world,

so why would one think anyone would pause to listen to black birds
jamboreeing high up in a mango tree in guadeloupe,
jabbering away about whatever in their jackhammer rhythms,
in a high-pitched language so insistent it seems close to frenzy

perhaps a poet like me—or you—would listen to that language
possibly holding mystery, magic, beauty, if only for clues
we may decipher from secrets these black birds might know—
the boasts of men—women, too—who are masters of the sarcastic
lingo of tongue-in-cheek put-downs, the wisdom saucing the air
surrounding the insistent slap of dominoes smacking tables—

what the language could offer up for me or you—if you are
out there—perhaps, is a thread, a possible connection, where
we might locate our spirits in a common, fertile space, where words,

language might be the glue holding communities together in place

Haiku Song

the sound of the wind
becomes the tongue of the voice
sung through poetry

A Vision

the star speeding across a midnight sky
is a voice in the shape of a glittering comet,
a bird burning as if it were pulsating
with a need of sex, as are these words carrying
a primal scream, hot & dripping with longing,

the star speeding across a midnight sky
is a voice in the shape of a glittering
bird burning as if it were a comet,
pulsating with the need to explode

Seven/Elevens

UNTITLED I

words are dice thrown across floors,
gambling tables, where language circumvents who
won or lost, comes down to bets
lost in chips when snake-eyes dooms your first throw, though
turn a seven, eleven
after bones stop rolling you dance as though great
music, love, entered your soul

UNTITLED 2

living in the world is mostly about chance,
the draw of straws, or cards dealt
in a game of poker, it's all about nerves,
how your eyes react in tight,
cold-blooded moments of chicken, will you fold,
cave in to raw fear, pressure,
will you become an improviser with chance,
probability living
inside this new moment offered you singing
as solo, the notion fresh
thoughts can carry art to new, profound plateaus

UNTITLED 3

walking beside a building
offers possibility of a falling
brick cracking your skull with death
coming in the blink of an eye, a dice throw
unfavorable to you
in that moment, the fickleness of chance, odds,
is an opaque, feckless risk

TOMAS

tomas came whipping in suddenly, winds howled
through wet morning darkness, wings
of cold rain, drenching voices swirling anger
from a roiling, angry sea,
tree branches kneeled down as if they were blessing
snapped sugar cane stalks, whirlwinds
tossing leaves, switchbacking currents, closed hands held
tight together as in prayer,
benedictions raised up to God to spare us
holy terror like this one
whipping hurricane winds in from Africa

UNTITLED 4

eye hear cold voices whipping
my language of poetry wet with snapping
syllables, flying off white
pages full of dreaming, whirlwinds of rhythms
trying to create a form
history can walk through as pure poetry
rooted in language of place

UNTITLED 5

poetry is form, draws from nothingness, song
seeking language to create
metaphor, meaning, a vehicle through which
words shape themselves into sound,
local elocutions mapping birdcalls, grunts,
slippage of puns, wordplays, jokes,
the march of history's impact on tongues, words,
the chance mixing of races
splices mestizo voices, tongues simmered down
in pots of creole culture,
food we eat today is language won or lost

UNTITLED 6

throw the bones again to see
where the dice stop rolling through life's chief moments
of chance, do they roll stopping
with snake-eyes, seven/eleven turning up
inside luck, ability
raised up from cultural fusion, risk, fresh modes,
language echoing the new

UNTITLED 7

poetic language rolls off tongues like dice throws,
words tumble through poems risking
they might fall off cliffs of sheer rock-face meters,
rhythms suddenly breaking
backs of sentences, veering in another
direction, alongside chance,
risk the only way to dance with creation,
expression, art, politics

in the hands of poets become high-wire acts
balancing cool survival,
creative voices walk through space, joyously

UNTITLED 8
snake eyes in eyes of hustlers,
pimps, who throw their lives into moments of death,
snake eyes in stares of lizards,
who slither belly-down through sawgrass, people,
snake eyes fixed in eyes of men
shooting bullets with their gazes, guns firing,
snake eyes empty of beauty

UNTITLED 9
on the first throw of words tumbling off tongues, risk,
chance takes over, becomes birds,
spreads wings, lifts off into space, is a solo,
music as air beneath wings,
breath of notes is a chance to where wind takes poems
in the moment art lives, thrives,
takes off as tongue when rhythm rolls as thrown dice
huck-a-bucking across floors,
carrying the sound of possibility
artists creating in air
carved out by miles davis, monk, jimi hendrix

UNTITLED 10
where is the courage to sing
songs no one plays over airways, radios,
television, internets,
where are great poets celebrated as news

anywhere in this country,
their poems & faces splashed all over TV
like that of sarah palin

UNTITLED II
it is late in the game when new dice are thrown
again, where did the risk go
with the early throw of the bones, time always
moves in the moment of now,
choices thrown across gambling tables become
the present voices, the new
throw of language as dice roll toward edges, chance,
risk, art lived in the margins
where great poetry creates in peril, loss
the name of the modern game,
is fame, the throw of cold dice, no matter what . . .

NOTE: I grew up in the inner city of St. Louis, Missouri, and I watched older and younger people—mostly men—gambling when they played the game of dice. Some were killed because one of their adversary's perhaps thought they were cheating, though sometimes it was for winning a great deal of money, which made their opponents mad. So in my mind playing the game of dice contains within its mandate an essential element of risk and chance. *Seven/Elevens* is my attempt to create a new form based on the roll of the dice and the elements of chance and risk embedded in that game. To put it simply the form goes like this: in the "seven," the poem is seven lines, with alternating seven- and eleven-syllabic lines, beginning with a line of seven syllables. With the "elevens," the poem is eleven lines of alternating eleven- and seven-syllabic lines, beginning with an opening line of eleven syllables.

In my view of the form the series of poems opens with the seven form, with the next form being an eleven, though I don't see the form necessarily conforming to this strict configuration. For me the idea is to write poems that address risk, chance, as the throw of the dice does when someone is gambling, because in my view life and living is always about taking risk. Even if one approaches life conservatively, there is no way to predict what will confront you while passing through the daily activity of breathing and living.

What's the Real Deal Here

has anyone noticed the gap between fame & talent
has grown enormous as the grand canyon,
empty-headed showbiz prevaricators
                            giving themselves obligatory applause,
pushing their own bad books on their own bad shows,
               grinning dimwitted wack-a-moles
pretending they know the difference
between a blowjob & giving some head,

why all this media hullabaloo over new immigrants
who don't look like old immigrants, why all this
mistrust of islam, blind acceptance of crusading christian "shock
& awe" wars, wall street kleptomaniacs robbing everybody blind,
putting iou economic sclerosis into everyone's bank accounts,
getting get-out-of-jail-free passes for all their criminal behavior,
these kerfuffles over lovers kissing full on the lips in public, false
hysteria over naked well-endowed females (handsome men too)
that has been going on nonstop for how many years now—
most seem to have forgotten marilyn monroe's nude photographs,
those seductive playboy, penthouse pinups—is it wholesale
attention-span disorder, widespread, historical amnesia,
exhibitionists have been swapping globs of slimy spit,
probing their tongues deep into open mouths like hard penises
plunging into hot you-know-what for umpteen years now,

but here some nitwits go again, getting bent out of shape over sex—
how do they think they came here, through immaculate conception—

they are the first ones to get busted for buying pornography,
like supreme court justice, big-boob-loving, freaky-deek
self-hating clarence thomas,

what about all these networks celebrating illiterate white hillybilly
bozos screaming hatred all over idiot tubes without wearing
their kkk masks or white robes, clinging to guns & bibles,
itty-bitty teabags dangling from their corny tricorner hats
like lynched black men hanging from tree branches,
decked out in all kinds of sorry paraphernalia, looking weird as lady gaga
seen stumbling around an airport like a drunk, looking foolish falling down
wearing her black giraffe-neck soda-bottle lobster-claw-
shaped platform shoes,

why do so many get rewarded for sensationalism, like andrew brietbart
croaking like some rabid frog, murder-mouthing bought & sold stupidoes
speaking gobble-de-gook, kool-aid slogans on hysterical cable
networks, will not get anyone closer to independence
from walmart nirvana, nor grant anybody freedom,

everyone has to take a long deep breath, check their long-
winded ignorance at the proverbial front door, get a grip

because in the end lasting beauty & truth will be recognized
in any language wondrous as the flight of a glorious eagle soaring,
in a song over the awe-inspiring land of the original ancestors,
who knew enchantment of mountains, rivers, lakes, forests,
who danced to rhythms of winds in their drums,
wearing sacred eagle feathers in their divine headdresses, hallowed
the flight of this magnificent bird celebrated in their consecrated rituals,
etched into the camera lens eyeballs of their native memory,

reflected in clear river mirrors—without cracks, or evil intentions
their wisdom rooted in mysterious, magical divinity,
these moments can enrich us when we see ourselves
enshrined in a language holding metaphors of profound river-
words necessary for a nation to swim in,
then we can lift off into a blue space

pulsating with an eagle's heartbeat,
a memory calling for survival

Errançities

for Edouard Glissant

I.

the mind wanders as a line of poetry taking flight meanders
in the way birds spreading wings lift into space knowing
skies are full of surprises like errançities encountering restless
journeys as in the edgy solos of miles davis or jimi hendrix

listen to night-song of sea waves crashing in foaming with voices
carrying liquid histories splashing there on rock or sandy shores
after traveling across time space & distance it resembles a keening
language of music heard at the tip of a sharp blade of steel

cutting through air singing as it slices a head clean from its neck
& you watch it drop heavy as a rock landing on earth & rolling
like a bowling ball the head leaving a snaking trail of blood reminding
our brains of errançities wandering through our lives every day

as metaphors for restless movement bring sudden change
surprise in the way you hear errançities of double meaning
layered in music springing from secret memories as echoes
resounding through sea & blue space is what our ears know

& remember hearing voices speaking in tongues carrying history
blooming as iridescent colors of flowers multifarious as rainbows
arching across skies multilingual as joy or sorrow evoked inside
our own lives when poetic errançities know their own forms

2.

what is history but constant recitations of flawed people pushed
over edges of boundaries of morality pursuing wars pillage
enslavement of spirits is what most nations do posing as governing
throughout cycles of world imagination plunder means profit

everywhere religion is practiced on topography as weapons used
as tools written in typography to conquer minds to slaughter for gold
where entire civilizations become flotsam floating across memory seas
heirloom trees cut down as men loot the planet without remorse

their minds absent of empathy they remember/know only greed
these nomadic avatars of gizzard-hearted darth vaders who celebrate
"shock-doctrines" everywhere ballooning earnings-sheet bottom lines
their only creed for being on earth until death cuts them down

3.

but poetry still lives somewhere in airstreams evoking creative breath
lives in the restless sea speaking a miscegenation of musical tongues
lives within the holy miracle of birds elevating flight into dreams & song
as errançities of spirits create holy inside accumulation of daybreaks

raise everyday miraculous voices collaborating underneath star-nailed
clear black skies & the milky eye of a full moon over guadeloupe
listen to the mélange of tongues compelling in nature's lungs in new york
city tongues flung out as invitations for sharing wondrous songs

with nature is a summons to recognize improvisation as a surprising path
to divergence through the sound of scolopendra rooted somewhere here
in wonder when humans explode rhythms inside thickets of words/puns
celebrating the human spirit of imagination is what poets seek

listen for cries of birds lifting off for somewhere above the magical
pulse of sea waves swirling language immense with the winds sound
serenading us through leaves full of ripe fruit sweet as fresh water
knowing love might be deeper than greed & is itself a memory

a miracle always there might bring us closer to reconciliation inside
restless métisse commingling voices of errançities wandering within
magic the mystery of creation pulling us forward to wonder to know
human possibility is always a miraculous gift is always a conundrum

The Mystery Man in the Black Hat Speaks

I am the spirit of the dead African man lost in the Atlantic during storms and murders crossing those terrible waters during the Middle Passage. My spirit though mixed in a mélange with blood of Cherokees and the spirits of Tom Ridge Tom Ross the Apache warrior Geronimo the Sioux Chief Sitting Bull and the Shawnee Chief Tecumseh and his younger brother Tenskwatawa the one-eyed prophet and a whole lot of others. I rise up out of the ground out of the rivers walk and cut through mist fog tornado clouds hurricane winds come out of the ground from cracks of earthquakes the flaming lava of volcanoes and come here to this Mississippi River not far from Cahokia where the ancestors came upriver from the gulf and built those pyramids there to spite the white man. So I double/cross through the upside-down question mark of this here shining steel arch down here on the levy of Sad Louis and emerge from behind the polished steel and come out to greet you here to bring you a message but I can see you ain't ready yet so eye done changed my mind and I'm gon' walk back through the roiling rolling fog and mist until you ready to talk to me righteously because I am the voodoo spirit of African Indian double-take of cross-fertilization here in this cruel conflicted place called America. I am the double-back winding swamp snake who can cure these tortured spirits living here in this hellfire & brimstone place if only they will listen to me tell them the righteous truth. But until then I will come and go as I please as I want to sliding through the night with my mojo bone and juba shaking feather and appear whenever and wherever it suits me in my black hat and black cape sometimes riding a black horse and carrying a black whip that is my tongue that cracks and slips through the language we speak like a black mamba snake I move fast as an out-of-control brushfire strike deadly quick as a drone's exploding missile and then I'm gone just like that in the blinking flash of an eye.

135

Wooden Mouths

in oaxaca, eye heard melodious syllables rolling
supple from mouths of wooden flutes,
they bring to mind caressing massages of caribbean alizes,
whispering rain showers, delicate as soft breath cooing,
easing from lips of sleeping babies, seductive as sweet tongues of lovers
probing moist & passionate inside mouths of people they adore,

eye listen as music from these flutes circle slowly, lyrical—
like fused bodies of lovers do doing the do—
serenading us through this fragrant, mysterious air

full of magic, in oaxaca,

we are gathered here around the venerable tule tree—
a tree some say is the oldest living thing on earth—
are shocked to see twenty-foot-high veins evoking giant anaconda
snakes roping down the tree's sides to the bottom of its trunk—
which legend says takes thirty people to surround with outstretched arms,
or a hundred people standing side by side, shoulder to shoulder—

its snakelike veins stretching skyward bloom a green bouquet
from its womb underneath gravel & sand loam,
where the mixe people say the tree took root from a walking stick
one of their gods planted here way back in the day—

it is magnificent, all these green leaves bunched on branches,
shaped into a gigantic emerald natural

afro hairdo, it is mysterious, absolutely stunning, magical—
& it is still growing next to the red, white & blue
catholic santa maria del tule church,
with its ornate spanish twin bell towers on display
conquistadors built back in the seventeenth century—
they show the influence of spain's islamic moorish roots—

eye look around & see growing next to the tule tree
round, transparent hairy plants they call the *old man's balls*
& think, perhaps, people were doing the do
underneath this wondrous tree back then, a woman's legs are
wrapped around a man's shoulders, or back, while he was busy
plunging deep around & around in her wet, sucking vicelike grip,
his two balls wrapped in the skin of a scrotum swinging steady
in hot oaxaca air, like replicas of steel balls in newton's cradle—
minus three—set in a frame on someone's desk,

now eye return to listening to the sighing music
rolling through oaxaca's magical air around the looming sacred
tule tree—many call it the *montezuma cypress*—& hear ancient
voices whispering bloody history into my ears, sighing
whispering & licking like a tongue probing

into the vagina opening of my receiving ear

The Legend of Pablo Escobar

for Elkin, who told me the story

they say pablo escobar still lives high in mountains
above medellin, around rio negre, in the village
where he was born in politically torn columbia,
they say he walks fields & roads there, when darkness falls,
tell me his spirit has grown large as the legend/myth
surrounding his name, that his eyes still glow bright
as two suns or moons in the valley of eternal spring skies
over medellin, the bullet hole in the center of his forehead
is said to be a diamond, or perhaps a shining gold coin,
they say he still prowls restlessly through the plaza
in rio negre, where he washed dirty cars when he was young,
when he weighed less than a small bag of bones,
or a kilo of the very best cocaine,
they tell me in whispers his gigantic myth is larger
than the greedy men plundering the colombian government,
they say he walks through the memories of simple people
dragging large sacks of coca leaves & money
that he throws into the air like so much confetti,

they tell me pablo escobar still speaks carro-bomba—
explosions—every night inside the dreams of everyone
that he whispers softly to his father & mother every day
where they still live in their simple house in rio negre,
tell me the peasants of rio negre still gather in secret places
waiting for him to come all the time, their hands spread

open, waiting for gifts, pots full of gold trinkets & money,
they say pablo escobar can't sleep at night,
tell me he is very lonely since his legend is not flesh
but the breath of words others speak, they say he can't feel
the ecstasy he craves because women can't feel his penis
seducing euphoria from them inside their memories of him
probing deep inside their grip of hot wet longing
since he is only myth, only airborne words others speak,
they tell me though his memory still speaks loud
carro-bombas when he flies through skies over colombia—
like a giant warplane dropping bombs—gliding
over mountains like a gigantic, mythical bird,

like the image of him floating in a painting of botero
with a golden hole in the center of his forehead

Just Think about It

just think about it sometimes all you need do is open
a door, walk through it perhaps out into open space,
walk into the world, whether it's cold, or warm, then go
whatever direction your mind of errançities takes you,
go quickly, or slowly, but move resolutely through this moment
with your eyes wide open, your wandering brain, but move forward
toward something perhaps you haven't thought to do before,
whatever it is let there be beauty in it spreading light, meaning,
open yourself up to new music, people, vistas, spontaneous
improvisations of the day, rhythms carrying possibilities to unlock
secrets of this moment, perhaps will lead you to look into things,
people you never focused on before you walked through the door,
perhaps the opening will reveal yourself to yourself—revelation—
perhaps now you might feel different for the rest of your life

Looking into the Future

eye have spent much time looking into the future
elusive as it is sometimes hidden
inside a word a poetic line a sliver
fracturing a fragment breaking away from a flowing
conversation bursting from what someone just said
within a bright moment of elucidation

then perhaps eye might come upon it outside
a lyrical color-field of phrases becoming metaphor
as in a poem creating itself in an empty space
a white page or a secret place inside
the brain a painting forming on a blank canvas

after all is said & done maybe it will spring from
some woman's face luminous with spiritual beauty
carrying a deep elegant élan beyond
what can be captured in any photo is only close
to human feeling the heart knows but cannot explain
on an empty page during the rapture of composing

poetry is as elusive as the future
when all you see is perhaps a trembling outline
suggesting a shape a direction you are searching for
a presence pulsating with what you hope
is luminous with a pure beauty your heart will embrace

inside a clear moment of elucidation
you might hear it in music swelling within a voice
filled with a magical spiritual beckoning
perhaps it just passed when you were distracted
inside a moment of confusion now it's gone
forever inside a fog of dissolving mist
where time exists in a state of forming questions
inside a dimension giving shape to nods flurries
winks blinking within intervals of expectations
moments on the verge of arrival music a kiss

something you have been yearning for all your life

Eye Travel Back into Memory

eye travel back into memory searching for voices,
faces enshrouded in fog, silence-filled roads
blooming with shadows waving their limbs
as tree leaves do dancing on concrete when winds come,
sweep through them with musical tongues speaking a language so
naturally some bodies understand as they move rhythmically
out on dance floors, somewhere someone is walking
secure in their space, they might be an artist, pure
essence inside a dancer's comfort zone, pace
controlling movement of a body, the way music responds
creatively to tempo, improvisational movement, measure—

as when tree leaves when whipped by wind tongues prance,
dance, in tempo, as now my journey back into memory
is a dance, my eyes searching ruins,
wreckage piled high (as bleached bones dug up from graveyards
remind of living people who always take in, never give back,
their hands constantly open to receive whatever is given,
their hearts always closed, though they are beating)

finally eye come upon high-pitched sounds of male crickets
rubbing their legs against each other somewhere out there
in blooming fog, the rushing sound of water clear as wind chimes
tinkling up ahead, in the distance, perhaps, mystery
waits in a man dressed all in black, a flat, wide-brimmed hat, also black,
pulled low, cuts across his forehead like zorro's,

he rides a black horse—eyes milky moons in a black sky—
& looks through me as eye imagine death would—
then eye focus my mind upon the wind chimes' soothing music
up ahead, in the distance—movement will always take me there—
in a heartbeat eye hear water rushing through reeds,
licking over rocks & grass, see the road winding up to enter
mountains densely canopied with trees like in belle basse terre,
on the western tip of guadeloupe, near the silent
volcano of soufrière, long dormant as voodoo is here,
silent on this butterfly island (though you hear drums
beating lately now when darkness falls, during carnival season
when eye hear synchronized hearts pounding inside transplanted
haitian voodoo worshippers, their rara rhythms zigzagging snakes
through streets of pointe-à-pitre during mi-careme,
their breaths blown through conch shells, dancing
inside movement of shango, papa legba, ogun, obatala, erzulie—
loas long underground here until now—the old african
gods rising up through voices of people—young & old—
thumping in time with their hearts, moving as one, inside
comfort zones of their bodies, here on this island)

out there somewhere someone is walking toward me now
through this blooming fog, they are coming secure
inside their own flesh, within their own space, their comfort zone,
their eyes bright as beacons probe through the foglike lasers,
whoever they are eye sense their spiritual presence,
know myself in them, looking back, moving forward into mystery,
magic, see them as mirrors of myself, even now, searching
back through this dense, blooming fog—when will it ever clear—
gloomy with wavering shadows slinking across the road forward,
they speak—the wavering shadows do—a language

like wind tongues, like singing birds, like my tongue sings sometimes
in poetry when responding to improvisation of any kind—music,
voices, the sound of car tires screeching, machine guns chattering
back & forth at one another during wartime—whenever
odd clues drop cunning bombshells into equations of speech—
words strung out into sentences written by juries, judges, reporters,
poets—revelation, surprise suddenly, as in a quirky chord
change, shocking in its placement, coming out of the blue
as when a new tempo is inserted into a composition, a performance,
comes with the need to improvise, then control has to take over

as in this split second after this blooming fog opened up,
suddenly a doorway there, eye step through into a clearing where
time stops, inside my memory, knowing somewhere out there
someone is walking toward me & eye will know them
when their spirit mirrors mine, the music of their tongue speaking to
me in a language eye know inside my comfort zone,
inside a language of our two hearts, beating as one

Untitled Dreamscape

eye relive that moment after first laying eyes on you,
once again in my mind—in that dreamscape
long ago—in the dream you were still stunning as eye remember,
the spiritual beauty shining in your face was as radiant
as when the light first caught you in my sideways glance,
then surrounded you with a blue-ray aura—
now—as then—you are deeply inscrutable,
mysterious as daybreak, or sunset—the interval between
those two called twilight, when our minds play tricks,
fool us all the time, when what we think we see
could be a mirage, an illusion,
a magician's dazzling sleight-of-hand trick,
a moment infused with sweet seduction,

as when you first undressed & eye saw you naked there,
your body supple as any eye could imagine,
so perfectly sensuous, your swollen, plum lips
so ravishing—as they are now, in this present rapture,
your tongue lathering my imagination down,
licking over the glistening honey of your pursed kiss,
an invitation, your mouth open, your curling tongue
beckoning my lips & tongue to suck your peeled mango breast,
your pubic hair a mound of sweet dark moss,
my lascivious thoughts focusing like a laser on
the ravishing sweetness eye imagined was there,

it was what eye remembered as eye reached out
to embrace you—when the lights came on
& the dreamscape vanished, poof, just like that,
wiping out your lovely, seductive likeness,
though the memory is still there—a longing,
a miraculous dream, mysterious
as ever, as now, your inscrutable loveliness
always beckoning, like a drug, an invitation,
so rapturous it calls out to me always, as now,
when eye am dreaming, you always beckon,
seducing me, as now, as long as eye dream

A Man Walks in Slow Motion

for Usain Bolt in 2008

a man walks in slow motion as through a dream,
above the sky listens to blue heat waves
rolling across the miracle of its deep expanse
as pulsating clove-rhythms of music come & go,
improvising as they please, voices sashay
through syncopated beats, dreams suddenly appear
naked & clueless all over the globe,

time dressed as a sleek jamaican thunderbolt zips
quick as a blink through shotgunned meter dashes,
cracking like a whiplash he flashes down chutes
of white-lined red lanes on a track, shoots like a bullet
through dazed sprinters bunched in an arm-flailing group
behind him dropping tears sprinkling like bombs
detonating in their blues-drenched dreams,

they watch the thunderbolt zap to victory in awe,
dashing their hopes of glory as he slingshots
across the finish line, suddenly he is their fear,
a lightning bolt/flash zapping through a blue sky
deepening above thoughts of the mumbling man
stumbling like a drunk inside slobbering,
flummoxed speech, where a poetic thought was just
chopped off (reminds of surprise in the eyes
of a guillotined head after the sharp blade slices
off the neck clean) quick as a laser beam

scalpel inside the man's brain, leaves him silent
as a rock looking mute at a coconut cracked
open rolling mysteriously by his feet

& the moment is heavy when the blue heat wave
surrounding him vacillates its rhythms of love,
just when an oscillating storm cloud appears above,
exploding the sky, darkening the pulsing music,
joggers get wet from God's sweat falling from the cloud,
then everything for the man becomes confusing,
flows, though syncopations still come & go as they please
improvising upon rhythms of speech

the man hears inside his frazzled brain words grooving now,
beats flashing quietly quick as blinking strobe lights
through his thoughts, he sees the thunderbolt zap—
a whiplash across the sky in a moment
of speed—then truth enters his spirit when he moves

as through a dream, walking in slow motion
as a breeze tongues in as a song in a voice,
the sun breaks through clouds again much brighter than hope
people swirling around chaos in the world feel,

walking through a dream a man hears music surrounding
his spirit, senses it syncopating end to end
through the day, chords whiplash athwart a lucid blue sky

as rhythms come & go inside heartbeats as they please,
around the globe smiles break light across people's faces,

replicate daybreak cracking through night's deep longing

Connections #2

I.

eye look out my window, see mangoes hanging sweet
on tree branches starting to block my view of the sea
as they grow larger, somewhere a man sits with a rifle
pointing it at someone's head or heart without sentiment,
without knowing who they are before shooting them,
in the same moment a bird lifts off a branch
where it just hatched an egg above the crouching man
who just pulled the trigger, now someone *else* who doesn't know
who the sniper is locks in on *his* head—X marks the spot
in the center of his forehead—with a rifle scope, pulls the trigger,
time is always changing across the globe, around the clock
seconds are constantly moving *tick-tock* about its face,
tick-tock measures time, moves the bottom line
of the balance sheet, what do we really know of shifts,
crack crack happening in miniseconds, onomatopoeia
clocking intervals brief is what senses recognize
when music changes tempo, rhythm moves the body,
somewhere else a fault line shifts the ground underneath our feet,
deep under the earth there is movement, violence we will not know
until we see dirt opening up in front of us, concrete streets,
sidewalks splitting, buildings shaking to rubble,
is a message from God connecting us all to an awesome, avenging
power, is an omen from a God we have never really known,
would not recognize if the Spirit sprung up in front of us

2.

what are the connections between people waging war,
who have never met each other in the flesh,
who drop bombs on people making love in their bedrooms,
drop bombs on children playing in their own backyards,
doom doom from somewhere high in the blues, *doom doom*
explosions because someone said *they are our enemies,*
who said what to whom, what did they do to us
we didn't do to them first before we *doomed* them
as in iraq, afghanistan, libya, panama,

why do they hate us so we said after blowbacks on 9/11,

there are connections that bind us each to our actions,
everywhere images cross wires in minisecond errançities,
somewhere some/body is a walking time bomb
about to go off, explode, do whatever it takes
to destroy, at the same time a climbing wisteria blossoms
a purple drooping flower around santa fe,
at the foot of the sangre de christos (blood of the Christ)
mountains, spathiphyllum, blue hydrangeas bloom
in the sonora desert, a brightly beaded gila monster looms,
slowly hunts for small animals, with a keen sense of smell
digs for bird eggs beneath evaporational graves,

where earth metamorphoses into fine grains of sand

3.

throughout the world there are people who know secrets,
balancing competing agendas they use words of yin & yang,
in the world all people are equally human,
everybody's heart beats in their chests like metronomes
until they stop, most things in nature seem symmetrical
inside their violent forces housing harmonious discord
as in an exploding volcano spewing lava is the seed for birthing land,
as a lioness runs down a wildebeest, killing it inside the serengeti
ngorongoro crater, a woman births a genius child somewhere in light
as an anaconda crushes then swallows a large dog in the amazon
& it all seems so asymmetrical until you consider
every living thing has to eat something for survival,
is perhaps an act of mercy rather than killing for malice,
revenge, or murder because of skin color, or something
equally stupid like torturing for worshipping different gods,
slaughtering entire families for fear of difference, anger,
with machine-gun fire

is different than flames devouring dream mansions
of those who live knowingly in danger zones,
where rivers flood, conflagrations rage through hot zones,
though pain is the same for these hearts who go back
to sift through ashes—their lives suddenly gone up in smoke,
swept away by surging rivers, tsunamis,
blown apart by hurricanes, tornado winds, earthquakes swallowing
lives cracked to smithereens by fear—as any other pain,
compassion is still here as an act of mercy when hearts embrace
the possibilities of love through healing

4.

during moments of deep pain some experience healing, resurrection,
perhaps feel them deeply in their hearts as a flash, like *duende,*
wisdom might pave the way to insight, beauty, a blessing, *duende,*
perhaps is a life-changing force as in the instant you know
death is truly possible, as daybreak will most certainly come
if there is no world-ending conflagration after darkness,
flowers at the bottom of the sky will bloom, *duende,*
in some place where two people will make love with their hearts,
children will be born, old enemies may embrace differences
& life will go on in harmonious discord until it ends,

perhaps this is all we can dream of, hope for,
a few moments when there is clarity in our lives,
instances of mercy that reveal beauty, truth, as in watching

the mango tree growing outside my window beginning to ripen,
delicious fruit hanging like swollen breasts from its branches,
blocks my view of the sea—though eye know it's there anyway—
& eye can be thankful high up in those branches birds still sing
joyously every day, my heart sings with them
every time eye hear their music, the moment my eyes open wide,
eye breathe in whatever the day brings, time full of holy acts—

duende—profoundly impacts these sacred connections
we have one to another, each to each,
these blessed gifts we share as in breathing

View from the 48th Floor of the New World Trade Center Building #7

Five Tankas for Todd Stone, painter

1.

late sky view through glass
from the 48th floor, see
lower manhattan

stretch & bloom across the sound
busy with boats criss-crossing

2.

water surrounding
the statue of liberty,
is what todd stone sees

each day he paints faith rising
ground zero into the sky

3.

buildings point fingers
as steel glass architecture—
structures full of dreams—

punch holes through low-hanging clouds,
reflect light when the sun smiles

4.
heliocopters
buzz like black hornets darting
around rush hour,

eyes mist when lights flash below
light the fountain of heroes

5.
the sound empties out,
lights pop through blooming dark wings,
spreading west to touch

staten island, zooms across
black water calm with voices

The Last Stormy Breaths of Irene

whiplash winds ride the backside of hurricane irene
howling her last blustery breath as she blew over
manhattan on the last cool sunday of august
2011, she moved through a gray sky tinged
orange red at warp speed—squalling blabbermouth—
her corkscrewing tail end trailing havoc as she cruised north-
east toward connecticut, new hampshire, maine,
blowing like a bomb into brattleboro, vermont,
raining so hard she turned quiet brooks into raging
rivers there that exploded down crevasses, ravines,
spinning tail end havoc trailing behind,
spun into canada—like a romance gone bad,
the beloved running madly down the street,
clothes flapping wildly—in the descending night,
the tattered remnants of irene's dying breath

Sentences

movement of time through the music of space,
eye hear a bell ringing blue in sentences,

the language spoken in sleep becomes an echo here,
a translation when written down on white paper,

in the air, when spoken, words seem like a dream
pulsating through ether in blue melodies of tongues

weaving inside sentences, saturated with local
idioms, carved from blues spaces by human breath,

sounds rooted in voices here evoke metaphors
coursing blood-deep, form ancient tribal gestures,

where words fixed in geographic locations repeat
through reverberating memory, bring recognition

ricocheting through a collective truth, perhaps
then language can evoke a shared history,

when sentences might mirror rhythms of drums
& a rising sun could birth a circle of love

COLOPHON

Errançities was designed at Coffee House Press, in the historic
Grain Belt Brewery's Bottling House near downtown Minneapolis.
The text is set in Garamond. Display fonts include Libel Suit and Long Cool Mother.

FUNDER ACKNOWLEDGMENT

Coffee House Press is an independent nonprofit literary publisher. Our books are made possible through the generous support of grants and gifts from many foundations, corporate giving programs, state and federal support, and through donations from individuals who believe in the transformational power of literature. Coffee House Press receives major operating support from the Bush Foundation, the McKnight Foundation, from Target, and in part by a grant provided by the Minnesota State Arts Board, through an appropriation by the Minnesota State Legislature from the Minnesota Arts and Cultural Heritage Fund with money from the vote of the people of Minnesota on November 4, 2008, and a grant from the Wells Fargo Foundation of Minnesota. Coffee House also receives support from: three anonymous donors; Elmer L. and Eleanor J. Andersen Foundation; Suzanne Allen; Around Town Literary Media Guides; Patricia Beithon; Bill Berkson; the James L. and Nancy J. Bildner Foundation; the E. Thomas Binger and Rebecca Rand Fund of The Minneapolis Foundation; the Patrick and Aimee Butler Family Foundation; the Buuck Family Foundation; Ruth and Bruce Dayton; Dorsey & Whitney, LLP; Mary Ebert and Paul Stembler; Chris Fischbach and Katie Dublinski; Fredrikson & Byron, P.A.; Sally French; Jennifer Haugh; Anselm Hollo and Jane Dalrymple-Hollo; Jeffrey Hom; Stephen and Isabel Keating; the Kenneth Koch Literary Estate; the Lenfestey Family Foundation; Ethan J. Litman; Carol and Aaron Mack; Mary McDermid; Sjur Midness and Briar Andresen; the Rehael Fund of the Minneapolis Foundation; Deborah Reynolds; Schwegman, Lundberg & Woessner, P.A.; John Sjoberg; David Smith; Kiki Smith; Mary Strand and Tom Fraser; Jeffrey Sugerman; Patricia Tilton; the Archie D. & Bertha H. Walker Foundation; Stu Wilson and Mel Barker; the Woessner Freeman Family Foundation; and many other generous individual donors.

To you and our many readers across the country,
we send our thanks for your continuing support.

Good books are brewing at www.coffeehousepress.org